Library of
Davidson College

TRANSFORMATIONAL AND STRUCTURAL MORPHOLOGY

STANFORD FRENCH AND ITALIAN STUDIES

editor
ALPHONSE JUILLAND

editorial board
JOHN AHERN
MARC BERTRAND
ROBERT GREER COHN
FRANCO FIDO
RAYMOND D. GIRAUD
PAULINE NEWMAN-GORDON

volume V

ANMA LIBRI

In Defense of Structuralism

TRANSFORMATIONAL AND STRUCTURAL MORPHOLOGY

ABOUT TWO RIVAL APPROACHES TO THE RUMANIAN VERB SYSTEM

ALPHONSE JUILLAND

1978
ANMA LIBRI

Stanford French and Italian Studies is a collection of scholarly publications devoted to the study of French and Italian literature and language, culture and civilization. Occasionally it will allow itself excursions into related Romance areas.
Stanford French and Italian Studies will publish books, monographs, and collections of articles centering around a common theme, and is open also to scholars associated with academic institutions other than Stanford.
The collection is published for the Department of French and Italian, Stanford University by Anma Libri.

459.5
J93t

© 1978 by ANMA LIBRI & Co.
P.O. Box 876, Saratoga, Calif. 95070.
All rights reserved.
ISBN 0-915838-33-8
Printed in the United States of America

81-5392

CONTENTS

FOREWORD	1
1 INTRODUCTION	5
2 ABOUT CLASSES, SUBCLASSES, AND SUPERCLASSES	11
2.1 About superclasses	13
2.2 Rumanian verb superclasses	17
2.3 Subclasses and/or superclasses?	20
3 ONE OR TWO CLASSES?	25
3.1 =ea verbs and =e verbs	25
3.11 About stress	26
3.12 About sigmatism	27
3.2 Stress	29
3.21 Accentual differences	29
3.22 The marked/unmarked hypothesis	30
3.221 The statistical argument	31
3.222 The historical argument	32
3.2221 The "trend" from =ea to =e	32
3.2222 *rămîne* and *rămînea*	35
3.2223 Analogy or hypercorrection?	37
3.23 *alúnec* but *alérg*	38
3.3 Sigmatism	41
3.31 Sigmatism as a lexical feature	42
3.32 Sigmatism as a phonological feature	44
4 SOURCES OF RIVAL SOLUTIONS	47
4.1 Models	48
4.2 Users	49
4.3 Facts	51
4.4 Criteria	52
4.5 Explanations	54
4.6 Goals	59
4.7 Labels	62
5 CONCLUSIONS	67
BIBLIOGRAPHY	75

FOREWORD

Some time ago when generative and transformational grammar was at its apogee and few dared challenge its tenets, I was bold enough, or foolish enough, to hazard the view that "a good structuralist morphology ought to be convertible into a transformational morphology and vice versa," an imprudent claim for which I was taken to task by several scholars. The present essay is an attempt to justify not only why I made the statement when I did, but also to explain why I persist in reiterating it years later.

I endeavor to do so by taking a specific question—whether Rumanian verbs derived from Latin verbs in =ēre and =ĕre are better grouped into one conjugation or preferably assigned to different ones—to explore *in concreto* the descriptive resources and explanatory powers of the "two rival approaches" embodied in the "structural" and "transformational" models of grammar. I begin by opposing the structural solution provided by P.M.H. Edwards and myself in *The Rumanian Verb System* to the transformational alternative supplied by Merritt Ruhlen in "Two Rival Approaches to Grammar: Classical Structuralism vs. Transformational Analysis." The main objective of this comparison is to determine whether and how the two approaches differ and, insofar as they do, to ascertain the extent to which the differences between them are substantive rather than "stylistic." Essentially I try to find out whether there is anything of consequence that one model captures in its conceptual network which the other misses, misrepresents, or distorts.

As a result of this comparison, I submit:

1. That many divergent structural and transformational solutions are rooted in incidental factors which have little to do with the models themselves. Rather than the result of differences inherent in the descriptive and explanatory capacity of the models used, these conflicting interpretations are the outcome of different uses made of models the resources of which are largely equivalent.

2. That this essential equivalence is concealed by differences in terminology, modes of conceptualization, and style of verbalization.

3. That at least on morphological grounds, there is little that can be conveyed by the conceptual framework of the transformational model which cannot be conveyed as well by the conceptual framework of its structural forerunner.

4. That in many instances, the basic assumptions of the structural approach are sounder than those of their transformational alternative, and that certain structural solutions fare better when tested against the transformational standard of "plausibility," in that they are more likely to duplicate the processes through which speakers produce correct forms.

This being said, the supra-title, "In Defense of Structuralism," is to be taken literally, that is, as a *defense*: our study endeavors to show that, at least on morphological grounds, structural grammar can do as well as transformational grammar, though not necessarily better. Rather than an attack on the methods of generative and transformational grammar, ours is a challenge to certain claims made by transformational grammarians on behalf of these methods. I should add that I do happen to believe that the transformational branch of generative grammar contains a number of questionable assumptions which owe their stranglehold on contemporary linguistics to the polemic virtuosity of their proponents more than to the soundness of the views propounded. But this is a topic better left for another occasion. What bears no postponing is a discussion of the fact that several of the tenets which have contributed to the originality of transformational linguistics are now in jeopardy. Unfortunately the prestige of the Chomskyan doctrine is still such that many of its challengers prefer to advance their views as new developments within the context of transformational grammar when they in fact represent "a return to pre-transformational linguistics." For my part, I would like to make clear that inasmuch as this study calls into question certain basic views of contemporary linguistics, it does so on behalf of doctrines proclaimed half a century ago by the Prague School manifesto, if not by even earlier historicist insights which transformational grammar endeavors to recapture in synchronic terms.

I wish to thank my young and talented opponent, Dr. Merritt Ruhlen, who read an earlier version of this study and made several useful suggestions; and Marsha Shankman, for a thorough stylistic revision and excellent advice.

1
INTRODUCTION

The issue at hand is hardly momentous: how to classify two relatively small groups of Rumanian verbs—less than one out of every six in the language[1]—which show similarities as well as differences between them. One group forms the Infinitive in =ea, the other in =e, and they are locked in a love/hate embrace inherited from their Latin ancestors in =ēre and =ĕre. These Latin verbs had become confused in the vernacular,[2] and this confusion was bequeathed to their Romance progeny.[3]

As always when linguists find themselves in this kind of predicament, they are likely to disagree: struck by the differences, some will assign the two sets to two different classes; more impressed by the similarities, others will group them into one and the same. The pros and cons of these conflicting interpretations were clearly stated and carefully weighed by the authors of *The Rumanian Verb System*,[4] who reached the same unexciting conclusion as their predecessors: the dissimilarities between =ea and =e verbs outweigh similarities and the two sets ought to be assigned to different conjugations. Recently, however, a talented young transformationalist, Merritt Ruhlen, took another look at the problem and concluded to the contrary: in opposition to a long tradition and without bringing forward either new facts or fresh insights, he decided that the two groups are better grouped

---

[1] Out of a total of 803 verbs in Juilland and Edwards 1961, 392 are =a verbs, 19 =ea verbs, 129 =e verbs, 259 =i verbs, and 11 =î verbs.
[2] Grandgent §399 and §402.
[3] Väänänen §314.
[4] Juilland and Edwards 1971.

into one and the same conjugation.[5] Annoying as this unorthodox view may be to those accustomed to the old ways, Ruhlen's interpretation doesn't leave much room for a good quarrel, as there is nothing irrevocable about either solution: if the two sets are grouped into the same class, differences between them can be accommodated by dividing the class into two subclasses; and conversely, if they are assigned to different classes, similarities between them can be duly accounted for by grouping the two classes into one superclass.

Not the stuff out of which big controversies are made, it would seem; yet there is more to the argument than meets the eye. It is Ruhlen's main thesis that the two interpretations are representative of "two rival approaches" to grammar, one a stand-in for aging structuralism, the other the champion of transformationalism triumphant. What is really at stake, Ruhlen never tires of reminding us, is something more momentous than the classificatory fate of two small groups of verbs in a relatively obscure language: it is the unquestioned supremacy of a certain way of looking at language.

Although one would hardly suspect from the critics' discussion that the solution he advocates has been examined and rejected in the study he criticizes,[6] Ruhlen does not hesitate to use Rumanian conjugations as a stick to beat what many thought was a very dead horse indeed, structuralism. But judging from his relentless criticism, one wonders: could it be that the structuralist horse is not so dead after all? Isn't the structuralist method predominant in many other disciplines, in anthropology, sociology, literature, psychology, history? And isn't structuralism advocated today by certain leading philosophers as an alternative to Marxism?

But whatever it is that upsets Ruhlen, Edwards and I must have brought it upon ourselves by committing an offense akin to *lèse majesté*: we didn't pay tribute to generative and transformational grammar, a doctrine which was born after the late forties, when *The Rumanian Verb System* was conceived; our study, fully elaborated in the mid-fifties, went to the printers in 1958; the first proofs were corrected four years later, but it took another

[5] Ruhlen 1974.
[6] Juilland and Edwards 1971, §3.32 and §5.2.

decade before the book finally appeared, after vicissitudes galore, in 1971. What happened in the meantime, the emergence of Chomskyan linguistics, is now history. But the delays along the rocky road of publication had given us ample opportunity to confront our findings with the new approach, to profit from its insights, and to comply with its requirements. Well, we did and we didn't, as witness the following passage from our Foreword:

> The generative and transformational models developed by Noam Chomsky and his followers have not affected the results of an undertaking which, although in part a reaction against the excessively static outlook of distributionalism, nevertheless bears the imprint of a "structuralist" orientation in the derogatory sense assigned to this term in recent years. Whatever the merits of Chomskyan linguistics in other areas, a transformationalist reformulation of our statements did not appear to yield additional insights in the interpretation of Rumanian morphology.[7]

That we had our chance and failed to take it seems to bother Ruhlen more than the number of Rumanian conjugations. What he is bent upon proving is that Edwards and I went wrong not so much because we analyzed and classified Rumanian verbs as we did, but because we persisted in presenting our findings in the conceptual framework of an outdated model instead of recasting them in the idiom of the day. We were wrong not because we relied on the wrong facts or used wrong reason, but because we processed our findings through the wrong model.

Ruhlen's persistent critique—several of his publications have been devoted to exposing the vices of structuralism and praising the virtues of transformationalism on the grounds of Rumanian morphology[8]—give me a second chance to reconsider the alternative solutions in a more concrete way. Years ago Edwards and I had to confront our structural model with a transformational alternative that had never been applied to the data we had analyzed ourselves. It was a somewhat abstract confrontation as we had to translate our findings into an idiom with which neither of us was familiar. Now that Ruhlen has supplied a genuine transformational version to compare with our own, I am more convinced than ever that the basically traditional interpretation we formalized years ago was the right one; and that the trans-

---

[7] Juilland and Edwards 1971, p. 7.
[8] Ruhlen 1973, 1973b, and 1973-74.

formational solution Ruhlen proposes instead, far from being an improvement, is a bad solution. Whether its shortcomings are a consequence of imperfections inherent in the transformational model or are due, rather, to the imperfect use made of the model, is a question I prefer to approach only after I have had the opportunity to show *in concreto* where, how, and why Ruhlen went wrong.

However, I must anticipate one of the basic flaws in Ruhlen's argument. Every solution of a particular problem can be verified in two ways:

1. Within the restricted perspective of the data under immediate investigation—here =ea and =e verbs—so as to establish similarities and dissimilarities between them and decide which are to be subordinated to which.

2. In a larger context—here, the entire Rumanian verb system—so as to determine whether the solution proposed for the part is also applicable to the whole and to other parts of the whole.

The distinction is decisive because, whatever the usefulness of the first kind of verification, its validity ultimately depends upon the validity of the second. To be sure, a solution which accounts for part of the data may prove incapable of accounting for all. The relationship between =ea verbs and =e verbs may be such that a framework devised for their exclusive benefit may be unable to accommodate the more complex relationships between other groups in the system. Redundant when applied to certain parts only, a more complex and comprehensive framework may turn out to be more economical in accounting for the dependences which determine the system as a whole.

If I seem to belabor the obvious it is because Ruhlen's hypothesis founders precisely on these obvious grounds. Whatever the merits of the solution he offers for =ea and =e verbs, it is a solution that cannot be generalized to account for the morphological properties of other Rumanian verbs. Having considered =ea and =e verbs as if they were the only verbs in the language, Ruhlen proposes a solution that may retain, given this truncated perspective, a semblance of verisimilitude; but as soon as the horizon is widened to embrace other relationships the inadequacies of the solution become apparent.

The distinction between intra-class and inter-class relations, between members of the same class and members of different classes, will guide our discussion, but in reverse. We shall first consider the structural and transformational solutions in the broader perspective of the Rumanian verb system as a whole, as if our task were to account for all the relations which hold between all the verbs in the language. In this preliminary phase we shall concentrate on the relations which characterize the verbs Ruhlen assigns to the 2nd conjugation and those he assigns to the 1st and the 3rd. Once the problem is situated in its broader context, we shall reexamine the rival solutions to determine how well each accounts for the relations between =ea verbs and =e verbs considered apart from the other verbs in the language.

2
ABOUT CLASSES, SUBCLASSES, AND SUPERCLASSES

By considering =ea and =e verbs only, Ruhlen never gives himself a chance to look at the raw data before filtering them through the categories of his particular hypothesis. As a result, Ruhlen is not only unable to perceive what the opposition is doing, he is never fully aware of what he is doing himself. What Ruhlen fails to grasp is that even within the restricted framework of his own argument, the solution he criticizes and the one he proposes as a substitute are formally equivalent.

The gist of Ruhlen's argument begins with a rejection of the structural solution advanced in *The Rumanian Verb System* and ends with a summary of the transformational alternative. Consider the introductory statement first:

> As I hope to make clear at once, the necessity for setting up 'super-classes' is a direct consequence of sub-dividing e-stem verbs into two conjugations. That is, the sole motivation for such 'super-classes' is to capture generalizations which the original morphological analysis has destroyed. (187)

And compare the following:

> As I hope to make clear at once, the necessity for setting up 'sub-classes' is a direct consequence of grouping e-stem verbs and ea-stem verbs into one conjugation. That is, the sole motivation for such 'sub-classes' is to capture distinctions which the original morphological analysis has destroyed.

Consider now Ruhlen's conclusion:

> An alternative approach, which would retain all such generalizations as hold between *vedea* and *face* and still mark the stress differences which distinguish the two verbs, would be to assign both verbs (in fact all e-stem

verbs) to the same conjugation, and then SUB-CATEGORIZE e-stem verbs according to their stress pattern. (187)

And compare the following:

> An alternative approach, which would mark the stress differences which distinguish *vedea* from *face* and still retain all such generalizations as hold between the two verbs (in fact all e-stem verbs and ea-stem verbs) would be to assign the two verbs to different conjugations, and then SUPER-CATEGORIZE them according to their similarities.

I have paraphrased Ruhlen's statements in order to bring out the fundamental equivalence of the structural and transformational solutions, which have much in common: both aim to account for similarities and dissimilarities between the two sets; both agree on what the *prima facie* similarities and dissimilarities are; and both consider that the more important of the two ought to be accounted for at the class level, with the less important pushed up or down one notch to the next higher or lower level of classification, i.e., classes and superclasses in one case, classes and subclasses in the other.

Considered in this narrow perspective, the main difference between the two solutions rests on different estimates of similarities and dissimilarities: Edwards and I were more impressed by dissimilarities; Ruhlen is more impressed with similarities: *The Rumanian Verb System* assigns the two groups to different classes and relegates similarities to the superclass level, whereas "Two Rival Approaches" groups them into the same class and relegates dissimilarities to the subclass level.

In fact each interpretation contains the other: the structural case for assigning the two sets to different classes becomes the transformational case for assigning them to different subclasses; and the structural case for grouping the two classes into one and the same superclass becomes the transformational case for grouping the two subclasses into one and the same class. Ruhlen's failure to grasp this fundamental equivalence sends him on a series of wild goose chases seeking to justify the contention that one interpretation "destroys" what the other "captures." The victim of his own rhetoric, Ruhlen skillfully manipulates labels to suggest that there is a difference where there is none: a model which accounts for facts on a level other than class level either "destroys" or "captures" depending on whose goose is being cooked. Clearly registered similarities ("generalizations") which the structuralist relegates to the level of superclasses are said to be "destroyed"; dissimilarities relegated by the transformationalist to the level of subclasses are said to be "captured." This is plain rhetoric: the structural solution no more destroys similarities because it transfers their classificatory impact to the superclass level than its transformational counterpart destroys dissimilarities because it exploits their effect at the subclass level.

The question, then, is not which solution destroys and which captures, but *at which level it is best to account for similarities and at which for dissimilarities*. If, by stressing similarities, one assigns =ea and =e verbs to the same class, sooner or later it will be necessary to tell the reader that there are also dissimilarities, to be accounted for at the subclass level; if, by stressing dissimilarities, one assigns the two sets to different classes, sooner or later the reader will have to be informed that similarities also subsist, to be accounted for at the level of superclasses. Each interpretation pushes similarities and dissimilarities one notch up or one notch down relative to the other: superclasses down to classes and classes down to subclasses (transformational solution), subclasses up to classes and classes up to superclasses (structural solution).

2.1 About superclasses

From the beginning Ruhlen zeroes in on superclasses as his main methodological target: they are, he insists, a "special apparatus" improvised to rescue similarities Edwards and I destroyed when we assigned =ea and =e verbs to different classes: "the sole motivation for such 'super-classes' is to capture generalizations which the original morphological analysis has destroyed."[1]

In fact, the function of superclasses is much more extensive, as they are the only classificatory device capable of accounting for similarities between forms assigned to different classes. If it appears to Ruhlen that the "sole motivation" for superclasses is to capture similarities between =ea and =e verbs, this is because these are the only sets he takes into consideration in framing his

---

[1] Ruhlen 1974, p. 187.

hypothesis. But whatever the worth of Ruhlen's argument against superclasses, he turns it into a double-barreled plea on behalf of the transformational solution which, he maintains, by not destroying generalizations early in the game, requires no special apparatus to rescue them at a later stage.

Considered in the restricted context of =ea and =e verbs only, the argument sounds plausible enough: superclasses are novel indeed, whereas the subclasses exploited by Ruhlen are common fare in the morphological description of hundreds of languages. But closer inspection shows superclasses to be as legitimate and as inevitable as the subclasses they presuppose and by which they are in turn presupposed. And the fact that superclasses have never been used before, far from betraying their special status, is evidence of the inconsistent way in which morphological classifications have been undertaken in the past.

Every relevant feature determines both similarities and dissimilarities between the forms under classification: forms similar in terms of a given feature are assigned to the same class, forms dissimilar in terms of the same feature are assigned to different classes. But forms similar relative to one feature may be dissimilar relative to another: one feature may assign two forms to the same class, another to different classes.

If all relevant features consistently assign the same forms to the same class and/or consistently to different classes, all possible classifications coincide: there is no need to hierarchize the criteria, no need to decide which are more important than others. Moreover, if the classes determined by different criteria are always coextensive, the system will have only classes, as none will cut across the membership of another to divide it into subclasses, just as none will encompass more than one class and necessitate postulating a superclass.

Problems arise when the relevant features do not yield coextensive classifications: one criterion may assign the same forms to one class, another to two classes, still another to three; if the number of classes is equal, one criterion may divide them evenly, another unevenly; when classes are both equal and even, their membership may not be the same. When one feature assigns the same forms to the same class, another to different classes, the linguist must choose between conflicting classifications by deciding which features are more important than others.

We shall not go into the theoretical and practical considerations which guide these choices,[2] but will simply assume that they enable the linguist to select the feature or complex of features which determine the main classes of the system. Of greater interest is the fate of the features subordinated to those which determine the primary classes. If secondary features which cut across classes are used to divide them into subclasses, what about secondary features which cut *in between*, those which encompass more than one class? If the classificatory function of dissimilarities between members of the same class is to assign them to different subclasses, what happens to similarities between members of different classes? The answer is that, in most instances, similarities between members of different classes are simply ignored. This is true not only of criteria too specific to serve in establishing classes, but also of criteria recovered at the level of subclasses: whereas differences between members of the same class are used to assign them to different subclasses, the complementary similarities projected by the same criteria are overlooked.[3] There is no theoretical justification for such an unequal treatment, no good reason why inter-class similarities should be discarded when intra-class dissimilarities are retained.

Logically classes come first, with subclasses and superclasses established next, in terms of criteria subordinated to those which determine the classes. Ruhlen's charge that superclasses are a "special device" for capturing similarities destroyed at an earlier stage is true, but only as true as the reciprocal charge that subclasses are a special device for capturing dissimilarities "destroyed" at an earlier stage. Both statements are in a sense valid, but we must understand in what sense. It is because every choice presupposes "destruction" inasmuch as every choice discards what it does not choose. But one really destroys only what one casts aside without retrieve: subordinated features are *not* destroyed *if their impact is recovered at a later stage of the procedure*.

---

[2] After decades of "taxonomic" structuralism, a theory of linguistic classification is still wanting. Among the distinctions which affect classificatory choices are: general/particular, large/small, equal/unequal, even/uneven, marked/unmarked, positive/negative, binary/ternary, etc. Practical considerations are tied to the purpose of the classification: an imperfect classification may be preferred to a formally superior one which is less suited to the intended uses. For various conceptions of "class" in linguistics, cf. Juilland and Lieb 1968.

[3] For examples see §2.2.

Every description which aspires to account for both similarities between members of different classes and for dissimilarities between members of the same class needs a "special apparatus" to rescue the features subordinated in establishing classes. Superclasses are indeed such a special apparatus, but so are subclasses: the structural solution needs superclasses to recover similarities between forms assigned to different classes, just as the transformational solution needs subclasses to recapture dissimilarities between forms assigned to the same class.

The question, then, is not which analysis captures and which destroys, but rather which best rescues the features set aside in establishing classes, and which fails to do so. The difference is that the structural solution, which deals with both subclasses and superclasses, has the resources to account not only for dissimilarities within the same class, but also for similarities between different classes; whereas the transformational solution, which reckons with subclasses but rejects superclasses, can do justice to dissimilarities within the same class but not to similarities between different classes.

Given this simple fact, why is it that subclasses are so common and so familiar while superclasses have never been used before? The reasons are largely practical: the purpose of every classification is to facilitate the manipulation of numerous forms which are grouped for this purpose into self-sufficient entities called classes. This grouping preserves the relationships between forms grouped into the same class, but severs connections between forms assigned to different classes: against the common background of shared properties, dissimilarities between members of the same class become salient, whereas similarities between members of different classes can no longer be perceived.[4] In other words, class by class processing does not prevent the linguist from noticing dissimilarities between members of the same class, the basis of subclasses; it *does* prevent him from

---

[4] Another reason for this inconsistent treatment is that the the classification procedure is conceived of as a progression from the largest to the smallest, from general to specific, from all forms to individual forms. Determining classes is assumed to be the most general operation of the procedure, with subsequent steps specifying the forms with reference to increasingly subordinate characteristics: classes come first, then subclasses, then sub-subclasses, and so on, until all secondary characteristics have been exhausted, which means that properties encompassing more than one class are unlikely to be considered.

noticing similarities between members of different classes, the foundation of superclasses.

To summarize: CLASSES account for similarities between members of the same class, for dissimilarities between members of different classes; SUBCLASSES account for dissimilarities between members of the same class; and SUPERCLASSES account for similarities between members of different classes.

We are now in a position to anticipate what went wrong with Ruhlen's solution. We have seen that there are essentially three kinds of classificatory criteria: those which determine classes, those which divide classes into subclasses, and those which group classes into superclasses. The trouble with the transformational interpretation is that after exhausting the first, it only haphazardly exploits the second, and completely ignores the third. To be sure: (1) Ruhlen relies on the vowel of the characteristic inflections to establish three conjugations; (2) he resorts to stress differences in order to establish a distinction between the marked and unmarked subclasses of his 2nd conjugation, to sigmatism in order to differentiate the sigmatic and nonsigmatic members of the unmarked subclass; but he overlooks the interclass implications of the same criteria which involve the 2nd conjugation subclasses with the full membership of the 1st and/or 3rd conjugations; and (3) he completely ignores the subordinated criteria which involve the full membership of the 2nd conjugation with the full membership of the 1st and/or 3rd.

To deal with these lacunae in the transformational interpretation, we must consider certain facts of Rumanian verb morphology which Ruhlen ignores, but which were clearly presented and fully discussed in *The Rumanian Verb System*.

2.2 Rumanian verb superclasses

There is little dispute about the hierarchy of criteria which constitutes the Rumanian verb system: thematic characteristic (suffixation, sigmatism, and morphophonemic alternances) are subordinate to inflectional characteristics; among the latter, "noncharacteristic inflections" are set aside, while those we have called "intermediate" (Imperfect 1 to 6, Gerund, Indicative and Subjunctive 3 and 6) are subordinate to "characteristic" ones

(Present Indicative and Subjunctive 4 and 5, Imperative, Participle, Perfect 1 to 6, and Pluperfect 1 to 6). Edwards and I extrapolated and formalized this hierarchy which was inherent in traditional practice.[5]

While agreeing that Rumanian conjugations must be established with reference to the vowel of the characteristic inflections, specialists disagree as to the number of conjugations these inflections determine. The question is whether the five characteristic vowels (=a-, =é-, =e-, =i-, and =î-) should be reduced and, if so, to what extent. At one end of the spectrum, Edwards and I maintain that they shouldn't, that five conjugations ought to be recognized; at the other end, Ruhlen argues that =é- should be reduced to =e- and =î- to =i-, to posit three only; in the middle, the Academy agrees to reduce =î- to =i- but rejects the reduction of =é- to =e-, and settles for four.[6] But before going into the number of Rumanian conjugations, we must consider the fate of the subordinated criteria. What happens to the noncharacteristic inflections? Have they been cast aside once and for all, or must they be retrieved at some later point of the procedure and reintegrated into the final classification? Previous analyses have ignored this question, and so does Ruhlen.

The six forms of the IMPERFECT exhibit one of two possible sets of endings, =am etc. or =eam etc. Ruhlen's 2nd conjugation verbs exhibit the =eam set (*vedeam* like *făceam* or *mergeam*) and form a superclass with the 3rd conjugation verbs which exhibit the same set (*veneam*), in contrast to the 1st conjugation verbs which take the =am set (*cîntam*) and form a separate superclass.[7]

The GERUND forms exhibit one of two possible endings, =ind or =înd. The 2nd conjugation verbs exhibit =înd (*văzînd* just as *făcînd*, *mergînd*) and form a superclass with the 1st conjugation verbs which exhibit the same ending (*cîntînd*), in contrast to the 3rd conjugation verbs which take =ind (*venind*) and form a superclass by themselves.[8]

[5] Juilland and Edwards 1971, pp. 71-72.
[6] Guţu-Romalo 1968, who coordinates thematic characteristics such as suffixation and sigmatism with inflectional ones, reckons with 10 classes, whereas Felix 1968 postulates 12. The extreme outcome of the tendency to coordinate all characteristics is found in Pop 1911, who, by also placing morphophonemic alternances on the same level, ends up with more than one hundred classes.
[7] Juilland and Edwards 1971, §3.131, §3.221, and §3.321.
[8] Juilland and Edwards 1971, §3.132, §3.222, and §3.322.

The PRESENT INDICATIVE 3 forms exhibit one of two possible endings, =ă or =e, which are systematically reversed in the SUBJUNCTIVE 3 forms. Ruhlen's 2nd conjugation verbs exhibit =e in the Indicative but =ă in the Subjunctive (*vede* and *face*, *merge*, but *vadă* and *facă*, *meargă*) and form a superclass with verbs of the 3rd (*vine* but *vină*), in contrast to 1st conjugation verbs which take =ă in the Indicative but =e in the Subjunctive (*cîntă* but *cînte*) to form a superclass of their own.[9]

The INDICATIVE 6 forms also exhibit two possible endings, =∅ or =ă, which are reversed with =ă or =e in the Subjunctive 6. Ruhlen's 2nd conjugation verbs exhibit =∅ in the Indicative but =ă in the Subjunctive (*văd* like *fac*, *merg* but *vadă* like *facă*, *meargă*) and form a superclass with verbs of the 3rd which exhibit the same endings (*vin* but *vină*), in contrast to 1st conjugation verbs which take =ă in the Indicative but =e in the Subjunctive (*cîntă* but *cînte*) to form a superclass by themselves.[10]

We have not yet exhausted the inter-class relationships overlooked by previous analyses. Those we have enumerated above, Ruhlen completely ignores; others he ignores only in part. The solidarities registered in the preceding paragraphs cut *between* classes and the ensuing superclasses encompass the full membership of two or more classes. But other subordinated features are not so accommodating, as they reveal solidarities between part of the membership of one class and the full membership of another. Ruhlen exploits these criteria partially, when he divides the 2nd conjugation into marked and unmarked subclasses; but he neglects the complementary solidarities between the subclasses of the 2nd conjugation and the other classes determined by the same criteria.

Consider STRESS, the subordinated criterion used by Ruhlen to divide 2nd conjugation verbs depending on whether their characteristic endings (Infinitive, Present Indicative and Subjunctive 4 and 5, and Imperative) are stressed (*vedeá*) or unstressed (*fáce*, *mérge*). Using this criterion, he "captures" at the subclass level a distinction traditionally made by assigning the two sets to different conjugations. What Ruhlen overlooks in the process is that relative to the very same criterion, the marked

[9] Juilland and Edwards 1971, §3.111, §3.112, §3.213, and §3.214.
[10] Juilland and Edwards 1971, §3.111, §3.112, §3.214, and §3.215.

members of the 2nd conjugation (*vedeá*) form a superclass with the verbs of the 1st (*cîntá*) and 3rd (*vení*), as opposed to the unmarked members of the 2nd (*fáce, mérge*), which form a superclass of their own.

Now consider that among the unstressed verbs of the 2nd conjugation 93 form the PARTICIPLE (which also provides the stem of the six PERFECT and six PLUPERFECT forms) in =s (*mers*), whereas the remaining 36, together with all the verbs of the 1st (*cîntat*) and 3rd (*venit*), form it in =t (*făcut*). Aside from dividing the unmarked subclass of the 2nd conjugation into sigmatic and nonsigmatic sub-subclasses, the same criterion assigns the nonsigmatic to an oxytone superclass comprising all Rumanian verbs except the 93 sigmatics which form their own paroxytone class.[11]

In the PERFECT and PLUPERFECT forms, the 36 nonsigmatics, together with the stressed members of the same 2nd conjugation (*văzui, văzusem*), substitute -u- for the characteristic vowel (*făcui, făcusem*), whereas all other verbs preserve the characteristic vowel, the sigmatic unstressed of the 2nd conjugation (*mersei, mersesem*), all of the 1st (*cîntai, cîntasem*), and all of the 3rd (*venii, venisem*). Besides reinforcing the unstressed class of the 2nd conjugation (-u- substitution and sigmatism are complementary), the same criterion determines a superclass containing the sigmatic unstressed verbs of the 2nd conjugation and the verbs of the 1st and 3rd conjugations, in contrast to a superclass which includes the stressed and the sigmatic unstressed members of the 2nd conjugation.[12]

2.3 Subclasses and/or superclasses?

With all the facts before us, it is easy to see why the transformational solution turns out to be the "ad hoc" one, devised for the sole benefit of Ruhlen's 2nd conjugation verbs. This solution, which accounts for similarities at the class level and for dissimilarities at the subclass level, cannot be generalized without grouping all Rumanian verbs into one and the same conjugation. To be sure, if all similarities were brought down one peg, from

---

[11] Juilland and Edwards 1971, §3.214 and §3.233.
[12] Juilland and Edwards 1971, §3.121, §3.122, §3.231, and §3.232.

superclass to class level, one would have to group together: (a) verbs of the 2nd conjugation with verbs of the 1st (Gerund); (b) verbs of the 2nd with verbs of the 3rd (Imperfect, Present Indicative and Subjunctive 3 and 6); (c) marked verbs of the 2nd with verbs of the 1st and 3rd (stress, lack of sigmatism); and (d) sigmatic verbs of the 2nd with verbs of the 1st and 3rd (preservation of the characteristic vowel).

Of course, one could avoid such inter-class implications by discarding subordinate criteria altogether, but then there would be no way to account for the differences between sets Ruhlen assigns to the same conjugation. Because the same criteria which divide certain classes group other classes together, one cannot discard superclasses without also renouncing subclasses, thus "destroying" the differences which underlie the marked and unmarked subsets of Ruhlen's 2nd conjugation. Criteria which distinguish subclasses implicitly project superclasses, which means that to do away with the latter but not with the former one must be willing to retain dissimilarities between members of the same class while ignoring similarities between members of different classes. Even if Ruhlen were prepared to be that inconsistent, he would still have to answer the charge that the transformational solution fails to capture important generalizations or, to use a phrase of his own coining, that it "destroys" them.[13]

[13] Concerning the cross-conjugational similarities which underlie the concept of superclass, Ruhlen writes: "I do accept—and I think most structuralists and transformationalists do too—one 'superclass', namely the superclass called 'VERB.' Indeed there are similarities between my three conjugational classes, some of which [J & E] cite in §2.2. The fact that each conjugation does not have an entirely different set of inflectional endings, that morphological neutralization is a common phenomenon not only in Rumanian but probably in all languages, is self-evident. Such conjugational similarities are in my view best stated on the level of VERB."

Unfortunately this won't do. Properties stated on the level VERB must be common to *all* members of this class, in contrast to properties shared by members of other classes such as NOUN or ADJECTIVE. Properties which characterize members of *more than one class* are stated on a level *higher than class*, and properties which characterize members of *part of a class* are stated on a level *lower than class*. E.g., if substantives and adjectives share certain properties in common, these are properly stated on the higher level of, say, NOUN; and if nouns, in turn, share properties in common with verbs, these shall be accounted for on a still higher level, say, LEXICAL WORDS (as opposed to FUNCTIONAL WORDS). But properties shared by certain verbs and not by others—e.g., whatever makes a verb an =a verbs instead of an =i verb—must be relegated to a level lower than verb, say, CONJUGATION. Moreover, why should a less important division based on the endings of the Imperfect (=am verbs vs. =eam) be stated on the higher level of verb when the more important division based on the endings of the Infinitive (=a vs. =e vs. =i) is stated on the lower level of conjugation?

This ruins another of Ruhlen's claims, that the transformational solution is more economical because it does not require superclasses. In fact it is *less* economical in that it resorts to one solution to account for the solidarities which hold between the =ea and =e sets, but requires another to justify the solidarities between these sets and others. Without resorting to a "special apparatus" equivalent to a superclass, the solution Ruhlen proposes for the 2nd conjugation cannot account for the similarities enumerated in the preceding section. The structural approach, on the other hand, offers a coherent solution which provides for both similarities and dissimilarities between classes, subclasses, and superclasses. Ruhlen has been misled to conclude to the contrary by a partial solution which fails to take into account the entire array of relationships which constitute the Rumanian verb system.

The difficulties encountered by the transformational solution underscore the merits of the structural alternative, which are generality and specificity. It is a hard fact of life, and of language, that the solidarities which determine a system do not always point in the same direction: one criterion constitutes two classes, another three, yet another five; one criterion groups the membership of one class with the membership of a second, another with that of a third; one criterion involves the full membership of a class, another the membership of a subclass only. A classificatory system which recognizes only classes and subclasses can hardly expect to account for conflicting solidarities, a task which requires the cooperation of superclasses. Although a system which allows the same form to belong to more than one class is theoretically conceivable, it has practical drawbacks; but there are neither theoretical objections nor practical drawbacks to a system which prohibits multiple class-membership while permitting the same form to belong to several superclasses determined with reference to several subordinate criteria. In the same way, current practice allows any member of a class to belong to several subclasses established by several subordinated criteria. Like all good models, the one outlined in *The Rumanian Verb System* proves to be both versatile and specific; and, at least in this context, Ruhlen's transformational model proves to be neither.

What do these general considerations contribute to our specific question, whether to group =ea verbs and =e verbs into the same class or divide them into two different classes? Where do these considerations leave the contenders and their rival solutions? To begin with Ruhlen, I'm afraid he has managed to impale himself on the horns of a painful dilemma. Having charged, on the one hand, that the structural solution destroys generalizations and, on the other, having dismissed superclasses as an improvised "special apparatus," he must now choose: either to ignore inter-class solidarities and leave himself open to the boomerang of his first charge, that of destroying useful generalizations; or to recover similarities between classes through an additional level of generalizations and leave himself open to the charge of introducing, under transformational garb, the same conceptual device he has rejected in the structural version. One way or the other, Ruhlen's case is severely damaged: he must either drop the charges levelled at the structural solution and renounce the methodological claims made on behalf of his own; or he must concede that, by applying his very own standards, the transformational solution is liable to even more damaging charges than the structural predecessor it was supposed to improve.

And where do these general considerations leave *us*? In a much better position, I'm happy to say, than where Ruhlen left us. Not only have his methodological charges proven unfounded, each of them seems to have ricocheted against the claims he has made on behalf of the transformational alternative. Ruhlen has charged:

1. That the structural solution destroys generalizations which the transformational alternative captures. It is now clear that, far from destroying anything, the structural solution registers an entire array of solidarities which the transformational solution ignores or misses.

2. That superclasses are an artificial device, a "special apparatus." It now appears that superclasses are as necessary and as inevitable as the subclasses by which they are presupposed.

3. That the structural solution is redundant insofar as it resorts to superclasses, whereas the transformational alternative is economical because it can do without them. It is now obvious that the transformational solution requires an additional order of generalizations if it is to account for similarities between classes.

4. That the structural solution must resort to ad hoc devices for the sole purpose of recovering generalizations destroyed by the establishment of classes. There is little question that the transformational solution is the ad hoc one, devised for the exclusive benefit of Ruhlen's 2nd conjugation verbs, a solution which cannot be extended to the inter-class relations described so well by the structuralist network of classes, subclasses, and superclasses.

With the perspective cleared of ideological obfuscation, the two solutions will have to stand or fall on their own merits. Superclasses are here to stay: even if one can do without them in accounting for the relationships between =ea and =e verbs, they are indispensable when it comes to registering similarities between verbs unquestionably assigned to different conjugations.

We can now return to our original question, whether similarities between =ea and =e verbs outweigh dissimilarities or vice versa, whether the two sets should be grouped into the same class (with dissimilarities relegated to subclasses) or assigned to different classes (with similarities accounted for by superclasses). This question will have to be settled on the basis of concrete evidence, and the answer will depend on how well each solution accounts for the facts.

3
ONE OR TWO CLASSES?

Presenting the facts, all the facts, and nothing but the facts is a crucial operation: if all the facts are not presented at the outset, if an anticipated hypothesis is allowed to interfere with their presentation, the issue will become clouded, the alternative interpretations obscured, and the chances for a correct solution are going to be compromised. It is important, at this early stage, to present all the *prima facie* similarities and dissimilarities between the relevant sets so as not to allow premature assumptions to distort the "surface" data which are the ultimate means for verifying hypotheses about "deep structure" configurations.

3.1 =ea verbs and =e verbs

Differences between the smaller =ea set and the larger =e set are as follows:

1. In the Infinitive, the Present 4 and 5, the Subjunctive 4 and 5, and the Imperative 5, members of the smaller set are stressed on the ending (*vedeá*), those of the larger set on the stem (*fáce, mérge*).

2. In the Infinitive, members of the smaller set end in =ea (*vedea*), those of the larger set in =e (*face, merge*).

3. In the Participle, all members of the smaller set as well as a minority of the larger take =t (*văzut; făcut*), whereas the majority of the larger set take =s (*mers*), a difference which also characterizes the forms built on the Participle, i.e., the Perfect 1 to 6 (*văzui* like *făcui* as opposed to *mersei*) and the Pluperfect 1 to 6 (*văzusem* like *făcusem* as opposed to *mersesem*).

4. In the Participle, Perfect 1 to 6, the Pluperfect 1 to 6, all members of the smaller set as well as the same minority of the larger substitute -u- for the characteristic vowel, whereas the majority of the larger set preserve it (see examples above).

The four differences can be reduced to two:

1. Verbs which exhibit the first difference also exhibit the second and vice versa: verbs stressed on the ending form the Infinitive in =ea, verbs stressed on the stem form it in =e; and vice versa, verbs which form the Infinitive in =ea bear the stress on the ending, verbs which form it in =e bear the stress on the stem.

2. Verbs which exhibit the third difference also exhibit the fourth and vice versa: verbs which take =t in the Participle substitute -u for the stem vowel, those which take =s preserve the stem vowel; verbs which substitute -u- form the Participle in =t, those which do not form it in =s.

In regard to the first two features, the difference is between all members of the larger =e set and all members of the smaller =ea set; in regard to the last two features, the difference is between 93 verbs of the larger =e set and the other 55, i.e., the remaining 36 of the larger =e set and all 19 of the smaller =ea set.

All 129 members of the =e set differ from the 19 of the =ea set in regard to the first two features, while 93 =e verbs differ also in regard to the last two. In other words, 93 members of the larger set differ from all 19 of the smaller in regard to all four features, while the remaining 36 differ only in regard to the first two.

There is nothing controversial about these reductions, except that Ruhlen would like to squeeze out of them more than they can actually deliver toward eliminating the differences between the two sets altogether. To reduce the first two features he invokes a phonological rule which leads nowhere; and he prematurely, to say the least, discards the last two features.

3.11 About Stress

Whereas specialists generally refer to =ea verbs and =e verbs, Ruhlen believes that he can eliminate the difference between the two sets by referring to them as stressed and unstressed:

Let us attack the e-stem verbs by observing, with J & E (104), that different thematic vowels in *face* and *vedea* are an automatic consequence of a PHONOLOGICAL rule which diphthongizes word-final stressed *e* (cf. *vedea* 'see', but *vedere* 'sight'), without preventing us from assigning these verbs to the same MORPHOLOGICAL class. (187)

Unfortunately, this obvious phonological rule leads nowhere, if not into a vicious circle. A rule which distinguishes =ea from =e verbs in terms of a stressed ~ unstressed contrast helps little when there is *no way of predicting which among Ruhlen's 2nd conjugation verbs bear the stress on the ending and which on the stem.* The two features mutually presuppose one another, the accentual status of the Infinitive being as predictable from the shape of the ending as the shape of the ending is predictable from its accentual status. Accounting for one accounts for the other, but here the accounting stops. To refer the segmental to the suprasegmental contrast is to declare one feature "automatic" with reference to another which is not.

That the rule solves nothing can be seen from the fact that no economy is achieved in the lexical representations by introducing it into the grammar: if =ea is reduced to =e to convert ved=ea in ved=e, as in fač=e, then the reader won't know whether to pronounce **védem* or *vedém, fáčem* or **făčém*. In order to distinguish morphologically between ved=e and fač=e one would have to place an accent on the ending of verbs like *vedea*, i.e., ved=é, or add "marked" to their lexical representation, i.e., ved=e *m*, which means that the difference eliminated by reducing =ea to =e is reestablished with the necessary conversion of =ea into =é or into =e *m*. All the phonological rule has achieved is to replace one symbolization for another, =e ~ =é or =e ~ =e *m* for =e ~ =ea, a reversal of a circular distinction which does not break the circularity. A third term is required, relative to which either feature or both could be predicted. There is no such feature.

3.12 *About Sigmatism*

The reader must also be made aware of the *divide et impera* strategy Ruhlen uses to bias the issue by a tendentious choice of examples:

Furthermore, except for the difference in the three forms mentioned above (i.e., inf., 1 & 2 pl.), the verbs *vedea* and *face* behave IDENTICALLY IN EVERY OTHER RESPECT. (187)

This seemingly innocuous statement is true or false depending on whether the reader assumes that *vedea* and *face* stand for themselves or are stand-ins for the two sets involved. Taken at face value, the statement seems to refer only to these two verbs; it is true, but hardly significant. But if *vedea* and *face* are taken to represent all verbs of the smaller and of the larger sets, then the statement is false. Indeed, whereas *vedea* faithfully exhibits the morphological properties of all members of the smaller set, *face* represents only *one out of every three* of the larger (the 36 non-sigmatics which substitute -u- for the stem vowel), but not the other two out of every three (the 93 sigmatics which preserve the stem vowel). To select *face* as representative of the larger set is to eliminate the third and fourth differences not exhibited by this minority of verbs. In other words, Ruhlen decided in advance that his arguments in support of a reduction no one else performs, will be accepted. Thus, by simply selecting *face* as representative of the larger set, he can state, without bothering to mention the existence of sigmatic differences, or to justify their reduction,[1] that *all* members of the two sets "behave IDENTICALLY IN EVERY OTHER RESPECT." If the reader can be persuaded that the *only* differences between =ea and =e verbs are stress differences, he will be easier to persuade that the two sets should be grouped together despite accentual differences which stubbornly resist reduction. In fact, irreducible morphological differences subsist between all relevant forms of the two sets.

The picture should be sufficiently unscrambled by now to reveal the real contenders: those who group =ea and =e verbs into the same conjugation must argue for the reduction of accentual and sigmatic contrasts by making these differences predictable with reference to some other feature or features; and those who assign the two sets to different conjugations must show why such reductions are not valid.

---

[1] For a discussion of Ruhlen's arguments in support of his view that sigmatism be discarded, see §3.3.

3.2 Stress

In order to group =ea verbs and =e verbs into the same conjugation, the accentual differences in the Present Indicative and Subjunctive 4, 5, and the Imperative 5 must be explained in terms of another feature: members of the smaller set are stressed on the ending, *vedeá*, etc., while members of the larger set are stressed on the stem, *fáce*, etc., *mérge*, etc. Because there is no feature upon which these differences can be predicated, Ruhlen's argument moves in several subsidiary directions:

1. First, he argues that because so few forms differ accentually, a solution assigning the sets to different conjugations would be highly uneconomical.

2. Second, he maintains, with the help of statistical and historical evidence, that accentual differences between the sets are not like those which oppose members of different classes but, rather, like those which distinguish the marked and unmarked subsets of the same class.

3. Third, he uses what he perceives as a similar accentual difference between subsets of =a verbs to discount stress differences between the sets.

We shall examine these arguments one by one.

3.21 Accentual Differences

Ruhlen's opening argument is that accentual differences between members of the =ea and =e sets are too "slight," that too few forms are involved to warrant assigning them to different conjugations:

> In addition to the prosodic contrast in the infinitive, there is a corresponding contrast in the 1st and 2nd pl. of the pres. tense: /vedém/ 'we see', /vedét^{s}j/ 'you see', but /fáčem/ 'we do', /fáčet^{s}j/ 'you do'. Setting up different conjugations is, I insist, a very uneconomical way of specifying the slightly different stress patterns of *vedea* and *face*. (187)

A charge against the structural solution more than a claim on behalf of the transformational alternative, this argument overlooks three other forms which differ accentually, the 1st and 2nd persons plural of the Subjunctive, and the plural of the Imperative: *să vedém, să vedéți, vedéți!* but *să fácem, să fáceți, fáceți!* or *să mérgem, să mérgeți, mérgeți!*. Ruhlen's excuse for omitting them is probably that they differ *in the same way* as the parallel forms of the Present Indicative 4 and 5. But this does not alter the fact that they differ, and is no excuse for discounting them. Accentual differences between the two sets, then, are not as slight as Ruhlen believes, as they involve six forms rather than three.

Moreover, the six categories in question are *all* the free categories in the system, with either stressed or unstressed endings, all others being either always unstressed ("noncharacteristic" categories) or always stressed (all other categories). Basically, Ruhlen argues that under no circumstance should verbs be assigned to different conjugations on account of accentual differences, even when all the forms which can possibly differ do so in fact.

Finally, Ruhlen's own prohibition does not prevent him from distinguishing between the marked and unmarked subsets of his 2nd conjugation *in precisely these accentual terms*, the only difference being that he makes the distinction at the lower level of subclasses.

3.22 The Marked ~ Unmarked Hypothesis

The main argument in support of the transformational reduction takes the form of a hypothesis which likens stress differences between the two sets to those of marked and unmarked subsets of the same class rather than to those of different classes:

> I will assume that the stress pattern of *face* is *unmarked*, while that of *vedea* is *marked*, despite the fact that a-stem and i-stem verbs share the pattern of *vedea*. (187)

In other words, =ea verbs with the stress on the ending are *marked* relative to =e verbs with the stress on the stem, while they are *unmarked* relative to all other verbs in the language which also bear the stress on the ending (=a, =i, and =î verbs). Conversely, =e verbs with the stress on the stem are *unmarked* relative to =ea verbs with the stress on the ending, while they are *marked* relative to all other verbs in the language, all of which bear the stress on the ending.

Insofar as one expects a higher frequency of unmarked forms, the hypothesis makes statistical sense, but only as long as the two sets are considered apart from other Rumanian verbs, and only if frequency is determined by the number of members per class instead of the more significant number of occurrences in representative texts. The hypothesis collapses when placed in the context of the system as a whole: since the accentually free forms of all other verbs bear the stress on the ending, Ruhlen's hypothesis postulates an *unmarked set* which includes only *one out of every eight* verbs, in contrast to the *marked set* which comprises *seven verbs out of every eight*. But even if =ea verbs and =e verbs are considered in isolation, the textual frequency of the "marked" subset is higher than that of the "unmarked" set.

3.221 The Statistical Argument

Curiously enough, Ruhlen's beginning argument is unabashedly statistical: "Several pieces of evidence support this hypothesis. First, there are fewer verbs like *vedea* than *face*," writes Ruhlen, who refers in a footnote to the fact that "J & E list 19 like *vedea*, but 129 like *face*."[2]

Let us first register some surprise that an author who questions the usefulness of quantitative evidence in linguistic analysis[3] does not hesitate to make use of a statistical argument in support of his thesis. But Ruhlen himself invites us to look in this direction. Because of his otherwise low opinion of statistical data, he overlooks evidence which could have spared him the embarrassment of a counterproductive argument. To buttress the hypothesis that =ea verbs are a marked subset of =e verbs, Ruhlen resorts to dictionary frequency (number of members per class), which attributes the same importance to forms used ten times a day as to forms used once in a decade; he should have relied instead on the much more conclusive textual frequency, the number of occurrences in speech or writing. As clearly indicated on p. 109 of the book he discusses, the total occurrence of the 129 =e verbs is 13,727, that of the 19 =ea verbs is 16,940.[4] The average usage of =ea verbs is 891.58, by far the highest of any equivalent group in the language, that of =e verbs only

[2] Ruhlen 1974, p. 187. For the same argument by Iordan, see §3.2221.
[3] Ruhlen 1974, §5, The quantitative aspect, pp. 188-190.
[4] Juilland and Edwards 1971, pp. 108-111.

106.41.[5] More simply, for every occurrence of an =e verb there are some 9 occurrences of an =ea verb, which explains the long-term resistance of this deceptively "weak" class to assimilation by a supposedly stronger class.

The fact that the =ea set is actually stronger than the =e set refutes, on statistical grounds, Ruhlen's hypothesis that the former is a marked subset of the latter.

3.222 The Historical Argument

The second argument invoked by Ruhlen in support of the marked ~ unmarked hypothesis has clear historical implications:

> Secondly, as the Rumanian Academy has noted, verbs like *vedea* tend to be assimilated to the *face* class. *Rămîne* 'remain' (orig. *rămînea*) is a well known example of this trend. Another example is *plăceá* 'please', which, while still considered 'correct in Standard Rumanian, is currently being replaced by *pláce* among the younger speakers. (187)

Insofar as marked forms tend to be assimilated by unmarked forms, the argument would support the hypothesis if a trend from =ea verbs to =e verbs could be ascertained. Moreover, since the phenomenon is still alive (Ruhlen considers the pronunciation of young Rumanians particularly significant), it can be claimed that, if not entirely valid for today's Rumanian, the solution which groups the two sets together will be true for tomorrow's when all =ea verbs have merged with =e verbs.[6]

3.2221 The "Trend" from =ea to =e. Unfortunately, Ruhlen was misled by the Academy into advancing an argument which reflects the general opinion of specialists:

> Modificarea cea mai serioasă a sistemului morfologic verbal o constitue trecerea verbelor de conjugarea II-a la a III-a. Se poate spune că nici un verb cu inifinitivul în -ére nu rezistă acestei tendințe.[7]

Specialized opinion notwithstanding, I contend that the main

---

[5] These figures are computed from Juilland and Edwards 1965, which ranks the first 5,000 Rumanian words in decreasing order of frequency, dispersion, and usage on the basis of their occurrences in a representative sample of more than 20,000 sentences totalling about 500,000 words.

[6] "Avem de-a face cu două influențe de sens oarecum contrar, dar care converg spre un rezultat comun: reducerea a două tipuri de flexiune la unul singur." Guțu Romalo 1972, p. 126.

[7] Iordan 1947, p. 126.

pressure is in the opposite direction and that tradition, schooling, and literary influence are among the factors which prevent =e verbs from being accentually assimilated by =ea verbs.

To begin with, Ruhlen overlooks evidence to the contrary, i.e., shifts from =e verbs to =ea verbs: *băteá, bătém, bătéți* instead of *báte, bátem, báteți*, parallel to *făceá, făcém, făcéți* instead of *fáce, fácem, fáceți*, or *trăgeá, trăgém, trăgéți* instead of *tráge, trágem, trágeți*, etc.[8] In explaining why he has found more examples which substantiate a transition from =ea to =e than from = e to =ea, Iordan falls back on dictionary statistics:

> Conj. II-a este foarte săracă în comparație cu a II-a (cam la fel stăteau lucrurile și în latinește). Și conform raportului de forțe, care-și găsește aplicare și în acest domeniu, învinge categoria cea mai puternică, adică cea mai numeroasă. Din cele aproximative 20 verbe ale conj. II, n'am găsit forme analogice după conj. III numai pentru *avea, bea, durea, putea* și *ședea*, care grație unor neregularități în flexiunea lor, își păstrează sistemul moștenit.[9]

This is a peculiar explanation, especially since the 2nd conjugation (=ea) is actually stronger than the 3rd (=e). It is paradoxical to be told that verbs with irregular paradigms have resisted assimilation, i.e., regularization, because of their irregularity. It is even more puzzling to be confronted with a class which is still going strong after supposedly losing ground throughout the history of the language: constant "losses" do not seem to have weakened a conjugation which was weak to begin with. The resolution of these apparent paradoxes is found in a number of factors which have misled specialists into postulating an =ea to =e trend when just the opposite tendency is stronger.

To corroborate transitions from one set to the other one looks for =ea verbs "misused" as =e verbs, and for =e verbs misused as =ea verbs. Bear in mind that the average =ea verb occurs 9 times more often than the average =e verb, a circumstance which gives the speaker or writer 9 opportunities to misuse an =ea verb for every opportunity to misuse an =e verb. No wonder, with so many more chances to substantiate a transition from

---

[8] Iordan 1947, p. 126.
[9] Iordan 1947, pp. 127-128. The same explanation is given by Guțu Romalo 1972: "Verbele în -ea, fiind mai puțin numeroase (vreo 20) suferă influența acestora din urmă: forme ca *rămînem, va rămîne, țineți, ar țîne*, etc., acceptate de limba literară actuală au luat locul mai vechilor *rămîném, va rămîneá, țineți, ar țineá*", p. 107.

=ea to =e, that linguists find more examples of this shift than the other.

The *written* character of the evidence contributes to lead specialists into assuming a trend from the 2nd to the 3rd conjugation. To be sure, all misuses quoted by Iordan in *Limba Română Actuală* are taken from books, magazines, newspapers, and letters. Now Rumanian orthography does not use accents to mark the position of stress: to determine the prosodic status of accentually hesitant forms one must rely on certain segmental effects produced by the suprasegmental presence or absence of stress. Among the six forms which bear the stress on either stem or ending, only the Infinitive is unambiguous, because the shape of the ending reveals that *vedea* is an oxytone (ve·deá) and *face* a paroxytone (fá·če). Unfortunately, it is often impossible to determine the status of the other accentually free forms, the Present Indicative and Subjunctive 4, and the Present Indicative, Subjunctive, and Imperative 5: does the spelling *mergem* stand for an oxytone, /mer·ğém/, or is it a paroxytone, /mér·ğem/? To determine whether the stress falls on the stem or on the ending, the stem must exhibit the kind of vocalic alternations which vary with the presence or absence of stress: a spelling *facem* is for a paroxytone (fá·čem), a spelling *făcem* is for an oxytone (fə·čém), an -a- signifying that the stress falls on the stem, an -ă- that it falls on the ending. Now, while the stems of most =ea verbs reveal the position of stress through vocalic alternations, those of most =e verbs do not. Apart from *bea* and *vrea*, which are monosyllabic in the accentually free categories, only *vedea* (and its prefixations *pre-* and *între-*) does not reveal the position of stress through vocalic alternations; all others do,[10] which means that misuses of =ea verbs are more than likely to be disclosed by the spelling.

However, less than one out of every six =e verbs have stems which show through vocalic alternations whether their accentually free forms are oxytones or paroxytones: compare *batem* for /bátem/ and *bătem* for /bətém/ with *mergem* for either /mérğem/ or /merğém/. To be sure, a spelling *mergem* is likely to be interpreted by the linguist as /mérğem/ when the writer may have /merğém/ in mind. It follows that only a small number of =e verbs can betray, through their spelling, that they are being misused as

[10] *apărea, cădea, dispărea, încăpea, părea, plăcea, tăcea, scădea, zăcea.*

=ea verbs:[11] no less than 108 out of 129 =e verbs can shift the stress onto the ending in five of the six accentually free categories without giving the slightest orthographic hint as to their misuse. No wonder that specialists, who rely so heavily on written evidence, have concluded that the main trend is from =ea to =e, when the actual pressure is in the opposite direction.

3.2222 rămîne and rămînea. To substantiate this hypothetical trend, Ruhlen invokes such forms as *rămîne,* earlier *rămînea,* or the presumably recent *place,* the replacement for the standard *plăcea.* I believe that, correctly interpreted, such forms prove little, if not the contrary of what Ruhlen intends. Rather than analogical reshapings of earlier forms, those variants which may go back directly to Vulgar Latin indicate no transition at all; while others are at best half transitions, the result of imprecise language which refers to conjugation changes instead of shifts in accentual patterns.

Although *rămînea* goes back to the Latin REMANÉRE, I doubt that *rămîne* is a reshaping caused by the analogical pressure of =e verbs. If not a hypercorrection, *rămîne* probably derives from the Vulgar Latin REMÁNERE, just as its Old French counterpart *remaindre,* which cannot be explained as an analogical reshaping of *remanoir,* a descendant from the paroxytone REMANÉRE, the etymon of *rămînea.* Because the Latin 2nd and 3rd conjugations were often jumbled in the vernacular, it is likely that *rămînea* and *rămîne,* just as *remanoir* and *remaindre,* are descendants of REMANÉRE and REMÁNERE.

The same is true of *place,* which may be a descendant of the Vulgar Latin PLÁCERE, and of French *plaire,* which cannot be an analogical reshaping of the Old French verb *plaisir,* from PLACÉRE. Compare also the Old French *taire* and *taisir,* descendants of the doublets TÁCERE and TACÉRE. But Ruhlen, following Iordan, substantiates an =ea to =e trend by pointing out that the younger generation uses pronunciations like *place* while the older still pronounces *plăcea.* True enough, but quite inconclusive, considering that *every younger generation,* even those of a distant past, probably used this same pronunciation because they

---

[11] *abate, atrage, bate, coace, coase, combate, conoaşte, desface, face, întoarce, naşte, preface, reface, retrage, satisface, scoate, sparge, străbate, trage, zbate.*

hesitated between the two variants more than the older generation, who had more time and training to internalize the "standard" conventions which keep the two conjugations apart. Ruhlen mentions that *place* is the form used by his young Rumanian wife, which does not surprise me, as I often had the opportunity to hear young Rumanians use *place* instead of *plăcea*. Alas, the young Rumanians I used to hear saying *place* are now in their fifties and sixties and they no longer hesitate. But this change does not take place as anticipated by Ruhlen: instead of shifting completely to the paroxytone of their earlier days, the youngsters of yesteryear have mostly returned to *plăcea*. Iordan and Ruhlen interpret the alternative pronunciations in strict chronological terms, as a break between past and future, when the gap is more of a sociocultural one between young and old, a phenomenon which starts anew with every succeeding generation. Rather than gaining ground with the passage of time, the paroxytone pronunciation favored by the young tends to recede, with *place* shifting back to *plăcea* as the young grow older.

Moreover, I doubt that there ever was a genuine trend from =ea verbs to =e verbs or, for that matter, ever a full-fledged verb *rămînea* exhibiting the complete paradigms of 2nd conjugation verbs, i.e., not only *rămîneá, rămîném, rămînéţi* like *vedeá, vedém, vedéţi*, but also **rămînut, *rămînui, *rămînusem* like *văzut, văzui, văzusem*. These Rumanian verbs are now, and probably always have been, a mixture of the descendants of two Latin conjugations, like the Italian *rimanére* but *rimasto*, not **rimanuto*.

Specialists clearly overstate their case when they speak of transitions from one conjugation to another instead of referring to changes in accentual patterning. To be sure, the "misuses" which underlie their conclusions only apply to the six forms in which the accent is free, the Infinitive, the Present Indicative and Subjunctive 4, the Present Indicative, Subjunctive, and Imperative 5, and do not affect the Participle, the six forms of the Perfect, and the six of the Pluperfect. There is no evidence that those =ea verbs which have shifted the stress onto the stem have also acquired the morphological characteristics of the majority of =e verbs, i.e., sigmatism and the preservation of the characteristic vowel, no trace of a *páre, párem, páreţi* also exhibiting a Participle **part*, a Perfect **părsei*, or a Pluperfect **părsesem* (like *spart, spărsei, spărsesem*). And if this be deemed unconvincing because =ea verbs are more easily assimilated to the nonsigmatic subset of =e verbs, consider that there is no reverse evidence of a sigmatic which, having shifted the stress onto the ending, has also shed its sigmatic characteristics, no trace of a *mergeá, mergém, mergéți* with a Participle *mergut, a Perfect *mergui, or a Pluperfect *mergusem (like *făcut, făcui, făcusem*).

3.2223 Analogy or Hypercorrection? Limited as the reciprocal transitions may be, a correct understanding of their dialectic will show that the interpretation of =ea verbs as a marked subset of =e verbs is questionable. The underlying assumption is that misuses of =ea verbs are caused by analogical pressures exerted by the more numerous =e verbs, and that misuses of =e verbs are the result of hypercorrective reactions to the previous misuses: for example, under the pressure of *face, plăcea* shifts to *place* which, when brought back to *plăcea*, takes along *face* by hypercorrecting it into *făcea*. It is my contention that the real process is just the reverse, that the transitions from =ea to =e are brought about by analogical pressures and that the contrary =ea to =e shifts are the result of hypercorrective reactions.

To be sure, the pressures exerted by the less frequently used =e verbs are not overwhelming,[12] while the reciprocal pressures to shift the stress onto the ending are much stronger, exerted as they are not only by the more frequently used =ea verbs, but also by =a verbs, =i verbs, and =î verbs, which bear the stress on the ending: cp. *fáce* with *vedeá, cîntá, vení, vîrî*. It is much more likely that paroxytones such as *face* shift to *făceá* under the influence of oxytones such as *plăceá* and that, when the reaction to restore *făceá* to *fáce* occurs, the original movers like *plăceá* find themselves hypercorrected into *pláce*.

Contrary to common opinion, there are good indications that the misuses of =e verbs occur in "exprimarea mai puțin îngrijită," the less inhibited popular speech, while the misuses of =ea verbs characterize "exprimarea *prea* îngrijită," the more self-conscious writing of the semicultured who strive to master the use of the literary language for social status. Stressing the

[12] See §3.331.

ending is "what comes natur'ly" in these categories while stressing the stem reflects the somewhat artificial mark of control and prestige enjoyed by people supposed to know the difference and who do their best to resist popular *laisser aller*:

> Trebue precizat că fenomenul [trecerea verbelor de conjugarea III-a la a II-a] caracterizează, deocamdată, numai vorbirea muntenească (în sens larg) şi, graţie prestigiului acesteia, limba scrisă, care exercită o influenţă puternică asupra Românilor culţi de pretutindeni, încît formele respective se găsesc, în proporţii variabile, la oricine (şi, mai ales, la tineri).[13]

If we are right in assuming that transitions from =e to =ea are the result of analogical pressures, and those from =ea to =e the consequence of hypercorrective reactions to these pressures, Ruhlen's hypothesis that =ea verbs are a marked subset of =e verbs is further undermined.

3.23 alúnec *but* alérg

Ruhlen's third argument for discounting stress differences between =ea and =e verbs is an argument by analogy. He believes that =a verbs are affected by similar accentual differences, differences which have never served as a basis for dividing these verbs into two conjugations:

> . . . the fact that the stem is stressed in *face* while the thematic vowel is stressed in *vedea*, presents no more evidence for setting up two conjugations than does the stress difference, in the present tense, between (say), *aluneca* 'slip' and *alerga* 'run'; /alúnek/ 'I slip' vs. /alérg/ 'I run'. (187)

Ruhlen is so impressed with this argument that he repeats it in a long footnote in which he complains that "J & E present no arguments why the specification of different stress patterns in *e* verbs necessitates distinct conjugations, while different stress patterns in *a* verbs does not."[14]

True, Edwards and I presented no such arguments, and we didn't because it didn't cross our minds that such patently disparate situations could ever be equated: one represents an infraction to the primary accentual rule, the other an infraction to a secondary rule; one involves the entire membership of a set, the other only one out of every eight of its members. But since

---

[13] Iordan 1947, p. 126.
[14] Ruhlen 1974, p. 188, fn. 26.

Ruhlen insists that we justify our decision, let us spell out the fundamental ways in which the two situations differ.

Two rules control the placement of stress in Rumanian verb forms: a primary rule which determines whether the stress is borne by the stem or by the ending; and a secondary rule which further specifies the position of stress in polysyllabic stems and endings. According to the primary rule, noncharacteristic forms (Present Indicative and Subjunctive 1, 2, 3, and 6; Imperative 2) bear the stress on the stem; all other forms are stressed on the ending. All Rumanian verbs, including verbs like *aluneca*, conform to this rule, the only exception being =e verbs, which bear the stress on the stem in the Infinitive, Present Indicative and Subjunctive 4, and in the Present Indicative, Subjunctive, and Imperative 5: *cîntá, vedeá, vení, vîrî* but *fáce*. Compare *alunecá, alunecăm, alunecáţi* with *alergá, alergăm, alergáţi*, both oxytones, with the paroxytones *fáce, fácem, fáceţi* as opposed to the oxytones *vedeá, vedém, vedéţi*.

According to the subsidiary rule, stems or endings with more than one syllable are stressed on the syllable closest to the boundary which separates them, the last syllable of the stem, the first syllable of the ending. All Rumanian verbs conform to the subsidiary rule except for 62 out of 453 =a verbs and 19 out of 251 =e verbs, which bear the stress on the penultimate syllable of the stem instead of the expected last: *alunec* /a·lú·nek=∅/ but *alerg* /a·lérg=∅/, *birui* /bí·ruj=∅/ but *tresar* /tre·sár=∅/.[15]

The difference between the two situations could not be more striking: *all* =e verbs break the *primary* rule; only *one out of every eight* =a verbs breaks the *secondary* rule. Having established the facts, we may now deal with Ruhlen's conclusion:

> Although their theoretical treatment is inconsistent, their descriptive practice is not. Stress differences are handled in the same manner, i.e., by indicating lexically those verbs which differ from the unmarked pattern. In practice, then, J & E DO assign all e-stems to the same conjugation. (187)

Ruhlen is confused because he has no clear notion of what belongs in the grammar and what in the lexicon, no understanding of how features symbolized in the morpholexical representation are exploited in morphological classifications. As we shall see in the following section, Ruhlen is under the impression that

---

[15] Juilland and Edwards 1971, §3.323.

features incorporated in lexical representations cannot be used to assign the symbolized forms to morphological classes, when, in fact, these are the only features which can serve such a purpose.[16] Here he mistakenly assumes that all features symbolized in a formalized entry word are to receive equal weight in the classification.

It is true that "stress differences in e-stems and a-stems are handled exactly in the same manner" insofar as they are both symbolized in the morpholexical representations. But it is not true that Edwards and I "assign all e-stems to the same conjugation," a *non sequitur* which is the result of Ruhlen's failure to distinguish between two different operations: (1) the symbolization of features in the morpholexical transcript; and (2) the ranking of the symbolized features for the purpose of classification.

All that is required of a feature to qualify for symbolization in the morpholexical representation is that it be unpredictable. But unpredictable features are not equally important when it comes to classifying the forms which exhibit them: features which characterize only one form may have to be subordinated to those which characterize, say, half of them. Certain unpredictable features are considered significant enough to determine classes; others are retained only for dividing classes into subclasses; still others are dismissed as isolated exceptions and play no role whatsoever in the classification.

The accentuation of both *face* and *aluneca* has to be symbolized because both depart from the accentual rules; but since there are different rules to be broken and different ways of breaking them, not all departures carry the same weight. There are generalized infractions of a primary rule by verbs like *face* as well as limited infractions of a secondary rule by verbs like *aluneca*. The first infraction may be used to segregate verbs which conform to the primary rule from verbs which do not, by assigning verbs like *vedea* and verbs like *face* to different classes; infractions of the second kind may be used to distinguish verbs which conform to both rules from verbs which conform to the primary but break the secondary, by assigning verbs like *alerga* and verbs like *aluneca* to different subclasses of the same class.

[16] See §3.31.

There is nothing unusual about the different ranking of such features, a practice common to every classification, including Ruhlen's. Certain inflections, e.g., the Imperfect, assign Rumanian verbs to two classes, the =am class and the =eam class, while others, e.g., the Infinitive, assign them to at least three, the =a class, the =e class, and the =i class. Now when Ruhlen decides that Rumanian has three conjugations rather than two, he leaves himself open to his own charge, that of treating inflectional characteristics inconsistently by giving certain inflections more weight than others: he uses the endings of the Infinitive to assign verbs to classes, but he ignores the endings of the Imperfect. We are guilty of the same kind of "inconsistency" when we assign *aluneca* and *alerga*, both of which conform to the primary rule, to the same class, while assigning *vedea*, which conforms to the primary rule, to a different class from *face*, which breaks the rule. Nothing of course, prevents us from distinguishing at the subclass level between verbs which also conform to the secondary rule, like *alerga*, and verbs which do not, like *aluneca*.

But this is another of those frustrating games Ruhlen plays so deftly because he knows that the accentual irregularity of *aluneca*, for instance, is unlike that of *face*: he divides the 2nd conjugation into marked (*vedea*) and unmarked (*face*) subclasses, while not dividing the 1st.[17] The difference between the two interpretations is not, as Ruhlen insists, between consistency and inconsistency, but between different kinds of "inconsistency": whereas Edwards and I exploit the accentual differences between *face* and *vedea* at the class level, Ruhlen relegates their differences to the subclass level; but neither Ruhlen nor we retain accentual differences of verbs like *aluneca* and verbs like *alerga* in the final classification.

3.3 Sigmatism

Having dealt with Ruhlen's arguments for discarding stress differences between the two sets, we must now turn to those he marshals for dismissing differences associated with sigmatism:

---

[17] The temptation is great to ask Ruhlen why "he presents no arguments why the specification of different stress patterns in *e* verbs necessitates distinct sub-conjugations, while different stress patterns in *a* verbs do not?"

93 =e verbs form the Participle in =s and preserve the characteristic vowel, whereas 36 form the Participle in =t and substitute -u- in the Participle, Perfect, and Pluperfect.[18] Considering that only =e verbs exhibit sigmatism and that all sigmatic verbs are =e verbs, scholars have used these features to justify a 3rd conjugation with sigmatic and nonsigmatic subclasses.

To group =ea verbs and =e verbs into one conjugation Ruhlen must find a way to dispose of sigmatic differences, to which end he advances two arguments: (1) sigmatism is a lexical feature and, as such, not a basis for a morphological classification; and (2) the occurrence of sigmatism is predictable relative to the last two phonemes of the stem.

3.31 Sigmatism as a Lexical Feature

Ruhlen's first argument is puzzling:

> The fact that all sigmatic verbs follow the stress pattern of *face* (never that of *vedea*) might rank as an argument for assigning *face* and *vedea* to different conjugations. A more economical approach, one which would maintain all of the generalizations holding for e-stem verbs, would be to specify lexically such e-stems as are sigmatic, and to further mark such sigmatic verbs as take t in the p. ptc. This is essentially J & E's method (although, we recall, the authors do posit two e-stem conjugations), where *spune* is represented lexically as /spuN^s=e/ (219) and *rupe* as rup^{s-t}=e/ (219). It would seem that even consideration of sigmatic e-stems provides no support for two independent conjugations. (188-189)

A perplexing *non sequitur*: the conclusion simply does not follow. Certain verbs exhibit features associated with sigmatism, others do not: Why shouldn't they be classified depending on whether they exhibit these features or not? Ruhlen reasons that because sigmatism has to be specified in the lexical representations, it is merely a *lexical* feature, thus incapable of serving as a criterion for a *morphological* classification. To realize how incongruous this line of reasoning is, consider that the classificatory properties on which Ruhlen relies must also be specified in the lexicon as 1st, 2nd, and 3rd conjugation, i.e., =a, =e, and =i, the vowels of the characteristic inflections. Were we to take him at his word, we would have to conclude that the features symbolized in his own lexical representations as 1st, 2nd, and 3rd conjugations are

---

[18] See §3.1.

"lexical" features and, therefore, "provide no real basis for three independent conjugations."

Ruhlen persistently misunderstands the relationship between grammar and lexicon, a relationship which Edwards and I tried to clarify by anchoring the distinction in the class/member dichotomy:

> The misunderstanding results from a failure to grasp the nature of mutually presupposing concepts, which do not lend themselves well to separate treatment: because classes and members cannot be grasped independently, it is difficult to distinguish dictionaries from grammars in those terms, as the two must deal with both classes and members. The difference between them is one of emphasis and orientation: *grammars establish classes by grouping together members on the basis of the formal properties they exhibit and with reference to the relations they contract; while dictionaries determine members by specifying their formal properties with reference to the classes established in the grammar.* According to this concept, formalized entry forms are *sequences of symbols of class membership*, the function of each symbol being to indicate the phonologic, morphologic, and syntactic classes to which the symbolized entries have been assigned in the grammar.[19]

Features represented in the lexicon are means of assigning forms to grammatical classes, and their inclusion in the representation is a clear indication that they are to serve precisely that purpose. Those features which can be handled exclusively by rules placed in the grammar and not in the lexicon, e.g., phonological rules, can*not* be used to assign forms to grammatical classes. Ruhlen was misled to conclude to the contrary by an imprecise use of "lexical" and by a stereotyped understanding of the relationship between grammar and lexicon which Edwards and I had tried to correct.

Incidentally, this explains why it is more appropriate to call entry words "morpholexical transcripts," as we do, rather than "lexical representations," as transformationalists prefer: forms are to be classified *morphologically*, not lexically, with reference to the sequences of symbols which introduce lexicon entries. Perhaps because of this difference in terminology, transformationalists have overlooked our efforts to specify the conditions under which phonological, morphological, and syntactic properties are retained for symbolization.[20] Hence the pervasive

---
[19] Juilland and Edwards 1971, pp. 30-31.
[20] For a revised version, cf. Juilland 1972.

confusions illustrated so well by Ruhlen's peculiar reasoning about Rumanian sigmatism.

3.32 Sigmatism as a Phonological Feature

The second argument for discounting sigmatic differences between =ea and =e verbs is based on a claim that these variations can be predicted relative to the final phonemes of the stems:

> Moreover, the dictionary entries used by J & E for *spune* and *rupe* are themselves unsatisfactory. Marking sigmatic verbs lexically makes the claim that it is an ARBITRARY subset of the e-stems which is sigmatic, when, in fact, Agard has shown that the sigmatic subset is PHONOLOGICALLY CONDITIONED, and there is consequently no need to distinguish sigmatic verbs from nonsigmatic verbs in the lexicon. (180)

Ruhlen is discreet about the phonological features shown by Agard to condition sigmatism, and for good reason: Agard has shown nothing of the sort. Let us consider the rule in Ruhlen's own reformulation:

> *e* stems which follow the stress pattern of *bate* are sigmatic if and only if their stem does not end in *m, r, rn, s, sk, at, ak, ek* or *ed*.[21]

On several counts, this is a very odd rule indeed. To begin with, it is stated in negative rather than positive terms, sigmatism being brought about by the *absence* of certain stem features.

It is redundant inasmuch as it is supposed to apply to all verbs Ruhlen assigns to the 2nd conjugation, including the "marked" =ea verbs which *never exhibit sigmatism*. To form the correct Participle, Perfect, or Pluperfect of an =ea verb we are instructed to check the final phoneme(s) of the stem against the segments enumerated by the rule, an exercise in futility considering that we know beforehand that it will *not* be a sigmatic.

It is artificial inasmuch as there is no conceivable connection between the sounds supposed to prohibit sigmatism: three consonants, among which one nasal (*m*), one liquid (*l*), and one sibilant (*s*); two clusters, one a liquid plus nasal (*rn*), the other a sibilant plus stop (*sk*); and four unrelated sequences of vowel plus stop (*ak, at, ek, ed*).

It is unnatural inasmuch as there is no plausible relationship between sigmatism and the absence of the segments enumerated

---

[21] Ruhlen 1973, p. 22.

by the rule, and conversely, none between the presence of these segments and the absence of sigmatism.

It has no explanatory power because it contributes nothing to our understanding of the Rumanian language, gives no account of the intuitions of Rumanian speakers, and provides no insights into the deeper structures of the language.

Finally, since it has no mnemonic or pedagogical value, Agard's rule is impractical: it helps neither the student nor the teacher of the language, neither the speaker nor the linguist.

We may nevertheless derive some benefit from this rule if we understand how it came into being. If one wants to show that two groups of forms, any two groups, are in complementary distribution relative to some feature, any feature, the following procedure will insure success. Isolate the forms of group A ending in phonemes which never occur finally in group B, and vice versa. These forms can be declared in complementary distribution relative to the last phoneme of the stem, and set aside. But in each group there will be a residue of forms ending in the same phoneme as forms in the other group, say -a and -a, thus breaking the complementary distribution. For the latter, move back one notch to the penultimate phoneme: some of the forms which end in phoneme -a will have different penultimates, e.g., -b- and -c-, and are in complementary distribution relative to the last two phonemes, -ba and -ca. But again there may be a residue with identical penultimates which break the complementary distribution, e.g., -da and -da. Move back again and follow the same procedure to find out if forms ending in the same two phonemes have different antepenultimates, in which case these forms can be declared in complementary distribution relative to the last three phonemes, e.g., -eda but -ida. If forms are still left in the two groups which end in the same three phonemes, continue the same procedure until no residue subsists. At this point, use phonological segments long enough to keep the two groups apart and declare any feature you wish to discount as being in complementary distribution relative to the segments.

Notice that the process of discrimination need not move from right to left, from the last phoneme toward the first, as it works equally well from left to right, from the first phoneme to the last. Now for this curious operation it doesn't matter which feature is discounted or which procedure, left to right or right to left, is used. But this "curiosity," on closer inspection, turns out to be nothing more than a truncated version of discrimination by *listing*, a fact obscured by transcriptions in reverse which stop after one or two or three phonemes, i.e., as soon as the two groups have been exhaustively segregated. If the membership of the two groups is relatively small and the forms sufficiently long, i.e., if the degree of contrastive redundancy is high, chances are that the process of discrimination will be completed long before the beginning or the end of most forms (depending on the direction in which one moves), thus concealing the "inventory" nature of the "solution." But with every additional position more forms are likely to be listed in their entirety: two-phoneme stems after the second position, three-phoneme stems after the third, etc., until all stems have been transcribed in full.

This technique underlies the phonological "rule" supposed to predict sigmatism relative to the nonoccurrence of certain stem-final segments. But any feature can be discounted by a technique which creates the illusion of a generalization which is, in reality, nothing more than reverse halfway listing. Instead of listing in full the stems that are sigmatic and/or nonsigmatic, initial or final segments are listed so that no two identical forms subsist in the two groups. The shorter inventory of segments is then chosen for easier reference and the feature of one's choice is "predicted" relative to it, positively or negatively, as the case may be.

Now this is the kind of rule *à tout prix* which gave American structuralism a bad name, the kind of artificial formalization for which structuralists incurred the transformationalists' wrath. Rules of this kind are not plausible, they have no explanatory power, account for no intuitions, provide no insights into deeper structures, in short, they are useless. That a structuralist should have formulated such a rule a quarter of a century ago is understandable; that a strong advocate of plausible and natural rules should endorse it now is very puzzling.

4

SOURCES OF RIVAL SOLUTIONS

What conclusions can we draw from this confrontation of alternative solutions offered by these two rival approaches to morphology, one structural, the other transformational? There is no question as to which is the better *solution*; but can we make the same claim on behalf of the *model*? Alas, no, at least not as long as a transformational version of the structural solution can be worked out without much difficulty, and especially not as long as the choice between the two solutions has so little to do with the model employed. The more significant question is whether there is anything generative morphology captures in its conceptual network which structural morphology misses. At least in the limited perspective of Rumanian verb morphology, the answer is that there isn't.[1]

Quarrels about models are like quarrels about religion: some people are fond of the old religion, others prefer the new. The younger generation tends to exaggerate the importance of the unprecedented, while the older is prone to idealize the perduring virtues of the familiar. Given such attitudes, over which science has little control, the objective is not to convert but to understand how basic commitments differ and how they agree. What is important is not that linguists end up speaking the same language, "transformationalese" rather than "structuralese" or

---

[1] Ruhlen 1973-74 contends that the transformational approach allows for the reduction of =î verbs to =i verbs, with the result that only three conjugations are reckoned with in Rumanian. In a forthcoming paper, I shall discuss his arguments, which are no more convincing than those he advances in support of the =ea to =e reduction.

vice versa, but that they understand each other's language well enough to know what the other is saying.

I see nothing wrong with assuming that certain things can be said better in one technical idiom than in another, even that certain nuances can be expressed in one idiom which cannot be conveyed in another. The task is to pinpoint the distinctions captured by the transformational alternative which elude the structural forerunner. In this essentially "linguistic" undertaking, linguists have largely failed. Although we disagree a lot, we often don't seem to know exactly what we are disagreeing about. Ruhlen certainly doesn't understand very clearly what his quarrel is with structuralism, and the reason is not so much that he can't understand the structuralists' language, but rather that he has difficulty with his own.

Whenever transformationalists disagree with a structural solution, they tend to assume that structuralists fail because they persist in speaking a primitive idiom which cannot grasp the sophisticated notions and subtle nuances conveyed by the more versatile and refined transformational idiom. But by now we ought to question to what extent rival solutions are rooted in the unequal resources of models or in the different uses made of these models, not to speak of different objectives, standards of evaluation, amounts of data taken into account, etc. Only after the ground has been cleared of these incidental issues can we hope to focus on the intrinsic resources of competing models to determine when and how and why one is preferable to the other.

The following remarks are devoted to the menial task of distinguishing by means of a few elementary injunctions, between controversies which have nothing to do with the descriptive and explanatory powers of alternative models and those which are inherent in the models themselves.

4.1 Models

A model should not be credited with insights which are not characteristically its own in the sense that they can be gained and stated with equal clarity and concision in the perspective of an earlier model.

The treatment of verbal suffixation is a good example of this prohibition at work. This well-known phenomenon induced certain linguists to increase the number of Rumanian conjugations by assigning the suffixed and nonsuffixed =a and =i verbs to different classes. After criticizing Valeria Guțu-Romalo, a structuralist, for this unwarranted interpretation,[2] Ruhlen continues:

> The generative approach I am advocating assigns ALL a-stem verbs to the first conjugation, and then lexically marks those a-stems which take -ez-. For instance, *lucra* would have the lexical representation /lukr-, 1 conj., m suffix/. Marking conventions would specify that /u suffix/ → /+ suffix/, and /m suffix/ → /− suffix/. (186, fn. 18)

What could be clearer than that? Here is one interpretation by a structuralist who postulates four classes instead of two, here another by a transformationalist who reduces the four sets to two classes. The conclusion seems inescapable that the generative approach, which recognizes two classes only, is more economical than the structural, which redundantly postulates four. The only trouble with this conclusion is that the solution Ruhlen credits to "the generative approach I am advocating" is borrowed lock, stock, and barrel from the structural analysis he is criticizing.[3] This is not the customary complaint that credit is not given where credit is due. The point is that there is nothing *characteristically generative* in Ruhlen's version, and nothing that has not been conveyed with clarity, consistency, and concision in the structural original.

4.2 Users

> *Errors committed by the user of a model should not be charged against the model itself, especially when the model has the resources to account fully for the data misinterpreted by the user.*

A good illustration of the pervasive practice of faulting a model for errors committed by its user is the treatment of Rumanian consonant palatalizations to which Ruhlen devotes a section of his study.[4] The issue involves the softening of consonants followed by front vowels or semivowels, a phenomenon amply discussed in every descriptive and historical manual as well as in hundreds of articles and reviews. Ruhlen nearly manages to appropriate this familiar change and to credit its discovery to the virtues of the transformational approach.

[2] Guțu Romalo 1968, pp. 203 ff.
[3] Juilland and Edwards 1971, §4.21, §4.31, and §4.34.
[4] Ruhlen 1974, §3, Aspects of phonology.

In *The Rumanian Verb System*, Edwards and I gave consonant palatalizations a static formulation (Item and Arrangement rather than Item and Process) and chose to follow the common practice of symbolizing with a capital letter consonants subject to alternances of this kind. We had good reasons for doing so, which we clearly stated and which Ruhlen ignored.[5] All would be fair and square if Ruhlen had argued that Edwards and I should have introduced a rule in the grammar which would have permitted the removal of capital letters from the morpholexical representations. But, as always, Ruhlen is after bigger fish. He seizes upon this occasion to suggest that what he mistakenly perceives as an error[6] is to be charged not against the users but against their model:

> One serious drawback lies in the fact that phonological rules have been eliminated from [Juilland and Edwards'] description. (183)

Now the truth of the matter is that our description, far from eliminating phonological rules, considers them an indispensable component of every morphological description: section 2.3, appropriately titled PHONOLOGICAL PREREQUISITES, is devoted precisely to such rules, both suprasegmental (§2.32) and segmental (§2.33).[7]

The real question, then, is not whether the structural model allows for such rules, but whether Edwards and I should have simplified the morpholexical representations by introducing an additional rule in the grammar. In fact, we were right to resist the lure of a facile generalization which creates more problems than it actually solves.[8] But granting for argument's sake that we erred, the fact that Ruhlen faults the structural model only confuses the issue.

To make the same point in reverse, Ruhlen's transformational solution fails to account for an entire array of relationships outlined in a preceding section.[9] This shortcoming, however, should not be imputed to the generative model which has all the resources necessary to introduce a level of generalizations equi-

---

[5] Juilland and Edwards 1971, pp. 141-142.
[6] There was no error. See §4.5 and §5.
[7] Juilland and Edwards 1971, pp. 57-67.
[8] See §4.5.
[9] See §2.2.

valent to the structural superclasses. Models should never be held liable for lacunae that are not inherent in their conceptual networks; nor should they be disqualified because their resources are not exploited properly, consistently, and exhaustively.

4.3 Facts

A solution which accounts for only part of the data should not be judged by the same standards as one which accounts for more or for all.

Rival solutions may differ not because of differences inherent in the descriptive and explanatory capacity of their models, but because of unequal amounts of data they strive to describe and explain: one solution may seek to justify all the facts, another just a few.

American structuralists were subservient to facts in that they favored a rigidly inductive method: the "input," at one end of the assembly line, consisted of raw data which, processed through a series of "discovery procedures," emerged at the other end as an "output" of formalized statements. Facts reigned supreme and no mere "hypothesis" was allowed to alter them. Bloomfield claimed as a major virtue of his "mechanist" approach a capacity to deal with the data without making any psychological assumption about their nature.[10] Several scholars protested against this epistemological naïveté[11] but none was more persuasive than Noam Chomsky in exposing the sterility of such confining objectivism. Largely as a result of his influence, American linguists gained new freedom in dealing with the data: the "inductive" method ceased to be compulsory, one could also proceed deductively, that is, start with a hypothesis and test it against the facts. It again became possible to shift back and forth between fact and hypothesis rather than proceeding unidirectionally, from raw fact to formalized statement.

---

[10] "In 1914 I based this phase of the exposition on the psychologic system of Wilhelm Wundt, which was then widely accepted. Since that time there has been much upheaval in psychology; we have learned, at any rate, what one of our masters suspected thirty years ago, namely, that we can pursue the study of language without reference to any one psychological doctrine, and that to do so safeguards our results and makes them more significant to workers in related fields", 1933, p. vii.

[11] Juilland and Elliott 1957.

This welcome, though not unprecedented, development—in the forties Louis Hjelmslev and the glossematicians argued insistently for a deductive approach to language—is not without problems of its own. Whatever the limitations of a strictly inductive method, it has the merit of compelling the linguist to provide all the *prima facie* evidence from the outset, thus making it easier to keep "fact" apart from "fiction." There is no easy way around testing generalizations against *all* the facts instead of a selected few. A deductive alternative remains unassailable as long as it confronts its hypotheses with all the relevant data. The danger lies in the latitude the deductive procedure gives to the linguist to select only those facts which confirm his hypothesis while ignoring those likely to weaken it. Consequently, divergent solutions may result not from qualitative differences in the rival models, but from the selection of data congenial to the contending hypotheses.

To be specific, Ruhlen's solution preserves a semblance of verisimilitude when applied solely to =ea and =e verbs, but his is a limited perspective which leaves out of the picture important solidarities between classes. The hypothesis disintegrates when placed in the wider perspective which embraces inter-class similarities and takes into account dissimilarities associated with sigmatism, all of which are duly accounted for in the structural interpretation.

The newly gained freedom may be abused: advantages claimed for a certain solution may be the result of excessive liberties taken with the facts, which leave part of the evidence out of the picture.

4.4 Criteria

Criteria exploited by one model should not be denied to another.

This is the old story of double standards: *Quod licet Iovi non licet bovi*. Transformationalists have been known to criticize others for relying on evidence they themselves do not hesitate to exploit for their own purposes. Ruhlen devotes section 6 of his essay to call into question the usefulness of statistical considerations in linguistic investigations. For instance:

> In defining competence as that knowledge which a person must be pre-

sumed to have in order to qualify as a native speaker, transformationalists argue that such a person need have NO knowledge of statistical measures at all. I find it hard to disagree with this viewpoint. (190)

Although I'd rather not argue about the elusive notion of competence, I will make a distinction between the knowledge a person must have to qualify as a native speaker and the knowledge a linguist must have in order to ascertain whether a person so qualifies. If statistical data have no bearing on the former, they have on the latter, as witness the errors caused by Ruhlen's lack of quantitative insight. Is "competence" involved in determining the marked and unmarked sets of a given class? Do questions of competence have any bearing on predictions about the evolutionary fate of linguistic classes? I suspect they do, but will refrain from any such discussion as long as we have no precise definition of competence. I *will* say that if Ruhlen had availed himself of the relevant statistical information he would not have made the mistakes he did. Had he considered that there are 9 occurrences of a =ea verb for every single occurrence of an =e verb he would not have declared the former a marked subset of the latter; he would have understood why a few =ea verbs have resisted assimilation by the more numerous =e verbs; and he would not have predicted that the two would merge in the future.[12] All of these incorrect deductions could have been avoided if checked against pertinent statistical information.

Transformationalists should make up their minds: either ban statistical evidence once and for all or stop badgering others for doing what they do not hesitate doing themselves. This applies not only to statistical considerations, but to historical evidence as well. American structuralists, whose descriptive traditions have been marked by the study of languages without a recorded past, were fierce about protecting the synchronic purity of the description. Locked inside the impenetrable shell of self-contained "corpora," Bloomfieldians banned historical evidence and ostracized comparative reference from every structural decision, operation, and procedure. Not so their European counterparts, who saw in "structure" a tool for unlocking the mechanism of linguistic change, a key to history, a principle of evolution.[13]

---

[12] See §3.222. For the same prediction by Iordan and Guţu Romalo, see §3.2221, especially fn. 6.
[13] Juilland and Roceric 1975, pp. 15-19.

The dynamic outlook of transformations, the method of generating forms and constructions rather than analyzing entities "out of the data," ought to be congenial to evolutionary considerations. But historical arguments have enjoyed a very mixed reception in transformational quarters. The transformationalists' reluctance to rely on anything that cannot be assumed to go on in the head of the contemporary speaker prevents them from taking full advantage of the insight that "the direction of historical change takes can give us some indications about the form of grammar."[14] It comes, therefore, as no surprise to hear Ruhlen reject the traditional interpretation which recognizes four conjugations in Rumanian with the disparaging comment, "under the influence of Classical Latin?"[15] What *does* come as a surprise is his use of straight historical evidence to support the reduction of the four conjugations to three: *rămîne* dates back to an earlier *rămînea, place* is used by the younger generation while *plăcea* is preferred by the older, and so on.[16]

But in most instances, historical considerations are reintroduced less obtrusively, under the guise of "natural" rules. Natural rules, as opposed to artificial ones, are supposed to reflect the deeper mechanisms of language, to express native intuitions, to explain the hows and whys of language functioning. When asked to be more precise, transformationalists answer that natural rules conform to the development of language, a contention they support by citing changes which have taken place in history. Fair enough, if they would preach what they practice, and refrain from castigating others for relying on historical evidence. The question of explanations discussed in the following section may shed additional light on this subject.

4.5 Explanations

"Surface" explanations expressed in contemporary idiom should not be preferred to real explanations presented in an old-fashioned style.

One major claim of the advocates of generative and transformational grammar is that their formulations explain mechanisms which elude their structuralist predecessors. But I submit that

---

[14] Darden 1974, p. 68.
[15] Ruhlen 1974, p. 185.
[16] See §3.2222.

certain transformational formulations are nothing more than relabellings of distinctions which masquerade as their own explanations, while others merely obscure and confuse the real explanations presented in the plain language of old-fashioned grammars. Some of these transformational "explanations" recall the ingenious method devised by Saint Exupéry's Petit Prince to bring about a perfect kingdom of law-abiding citizens: no sooner did one of his subjects break a law but the benevolent Prince issued a decree enjoining the culprit to behave exactly as he had. The very device contrived by our young but enlightened ruler to convert his realm into a perfect kingdom is used by transformationalists to convert idiosyncratic languages into perfect languages: as soon as a rebarbative form or construction does not conform to rule, the grammarian king decrees a new rule—albeit "minor" or "crazy" or "singular"—which declares the aberrant behavior lawful, so that whatever happens happens according to law and everything is *pour le mieux dans le meilleur des mondes*.[17] Shades of Epictetus and Spinoza! But John Ohala says it all:

> These [orthodox transformational] phonologists, for example, may notice that one group of sounds do one thing whereas another group does the opposite. But rather than seek an explanation for this difference in behavior they tack on different labels on the two groups, X and not-X (("plus the rule" or "minus the rule")), and then "explain" the behavior of a given sound or the whole group of sounds as being due to the fact that they are "X" (or "not-X"). The label, "X", of course has to be an undefined term with no empirical content, e.g., strength, chromaticity, bleaching, sonority, or syllabicity (as it is applied to individual speech segments). The progress of a field is inhibited when labels are offered as explanations. It is far preferable to simply admit "things happen this way but I don't know why."[18]

So much for explanations which are not real explanations. But Ruhlen's *pièce de résistance* is his solution for the softening of certain Rumanian consonants when they are followed by a palatal sound. Ruhlen formulates a rule according to which a palatal vowel, semivowel, or consonant turns a preceding s into $š$: "/ s → š/ → (t(r)) + /i, i, č/." But buried in a discreet footnote, "We face the problem that s is palatalized before i only when a mor-

---

[17] The same point is made by Herbert Izzo in an unpublished paper entitled "Pre-Latin Change and Sound Changes in Romance: The Case of Old Spanish /h/."
[18] Ohala 1974, pp. 351-353.

pheme boundary intervenes (cf. phonological /sigur/ 'sure' yields /sigur/ not */šigur/, . . .)."[19]

Unfortunately, this restriction cannot save the rule because Rumanian has an abundance of forms in which s, not ș, is separated from a following *i* or *j* by a morpheme boundary: *cos-iță, des-iș, folos-itor, impres-ie (-iona, -ionant, -ionabil), mis-iune (-ionar) mis-ivă, pas-iune (-ional, -iv), prisos-ința*, etc. Perhaps the rule could be salvaged by restricting it to forms in which an *s* is separated from the following palatal by an *inflectional* boundary, thus blocking the palatalization in forms like the preceding ones. Alas, not even this stipulation covers forms such as *găs=i, găs=im, găs=iți, găs=ind, găs=ii, găs=isem*, etc. The rule can be "saved" only by lexical exception, that is, by adding to the morpholexical representations of forms such as *găsi* the stipulation "minus the rule." But this is, in effect, to say that the rule cannot be saved at all.

The predicament of the transformational solution is well summarized by three related forms: the adjective *gras* "fat," the noun *grăsime* "fat," and the verb *îngrășa* "fatten." No palatalization rule can cope with a situation in which palatalization fails to take place before a palatal (*grăsime*), while taking place before a nonpalatal (*îngrășa*).

To fully understand the situation consider it in an old-fashioned perspective. Consonant palatalization was active in late Latin and early Rumanian. While it lasted, palatalization affected all forms containing an *s* followed by a palatal regardless of whether the two were separated by a grammatical boundary or not, and regardless of the nature of the boundary (between root and root, root and affix, root and inflection, affix and inflection). But the phenomenon was quickly spent and ceased altering prepalatal consonants which entered the language after the active period was over:

1. Inherited words in which the /si/ or /sj/ sequences do not date back to Latin but were created in Rumanian by a subsequent change such as e > i: *simți* rather than **șimți* (Lat. SENTIRE), *sigur* rather than **șigur* (Lat. SECURUS), *sine* rather than **șine* (Lat. SE + NE), etc.

2. Words created in Rumanian by a process of derivation: *desiș*

---

[19] Ruhlen 1974, p. 192, fn. 9.

rather than *deșiș (DES + -IȘ), grăsime rather than *grăşime (GRAS + -IME), folositor rather than *folosițor (FOLOS + -ITOR), etc.

3. Words borrowed from other languages: găsi rather than *găși (Sl. GASATI), impresiona rather than *împreșiona (Fr. IMPRESSIONER), pasiv rather than *pașiv (Lat. PASSIVUS), etc.

However, as Pușcariu has shown in an enlightening study,[20] Rumanian has exploited what was at first a purely phonological phenomenon to reinforce, by thematic hard/soft contrasts, certain grammatical distinctions such as person, gender, number, and case which were expressed in Latin exclusively by inflectional contrasts. Thus, the phenomenon of consonant palatalization has been kept partially alive in that the final consonants of stems which entered the language after palatalization ceased being active still remain subject to prepalatal softening.[21]

This old-fashioned account tells us why the transformational rule applies to the inherited stock (*și*) and not to either morphological innovations (*desiș*) or lexical innovations (*găsi*). It also explains the exceptions in both categories: why certain inherited forms, which developed the sequence after palatalization ceased being active, still show *unsoftened* palatal *s*'s (*simți*), and why certain loan words, which reinforce grammatical distinctions by hard/soft contrasts, show *softened* prepalatal *s*'s (*miroși*). The historical outlook clarifies *grăsime* (derived in Rumanian) as well as *îngrășa* (inherited from the Latin *INGRASSIARE).

The traditional perspective also shows how the transformational approach obscures and distorts by using a phonological rule to account for phenomena in which phonological, lexical, and grammatical factors are intertwined: (1) *phonological* factors account for the softening in forms present in the language when the phenomenon became active, i.e., inherited from Latin; (2) *lexical* factors account for the nonsoftening in forms which entered the language after the phenomenon became extinct: (a) inherited words which developed the sequence through a subsequent change; (b) words created in Rumanian by a process of derivation; (c) words borrowed from other languages; and (3)

[20] Pușcariu 1940, pp. 42-43.
[21] Compare also *îndesa*, with a nonsoftened sibilant, and *îngrășa*, with a softened one, both before the same vowel. The explanation is that *îndesa* is a parasynthetic formation derived from the Rumanian adjective *des*, whereas *îngrășa* derives not from Rumanian *gras*, but directly from the Latin *INGRASSIARE.

grammatical factors account for the continued softening in certain categories.

The "generative" rule could be saved only if there were some phonological or grammatical feature enabling us to predict which prepalatal *s*'s soften and which do not. Since there is no such feature, no rule placed in the grammar can spare the linguist individual specification in the lexicon: to produce correct forms, "minus the rule" has to be appended to the lexical representation of each and every form which does not soften a prepalatal *s*. But all this new solution achieves relative to its structural predecessor is to *reverse the marked/unmarked terms of an equation which remains the same*. To be sure, Edwards and I assume that prepalatal *s*'s remain unchanged unless otherwise indicated by a capital letter in the morpholexical transcript; whereas Ruhlen assumes that prepalatal *s*'s soften unless otherwise stipulated in the lexical representation by "minus the rule." Unfortunately, there is no other way out for ahistorical models of grammar which avoid *chronological* distinctions between forms having entered the language before or after a certain phenomenon took place, and reject *etymological* distinctions between forms inherited from the mother tongue and forms created in the language or borrowed from other idioms. This is why both the structural and transformational models must use lexical rather than grammatical solutions to cope with such situations.

Since the two solutions are formally equivalent, the only question is how to decide which is the marked and which the unmarked term of the distinction: the structural solution "marks" the *s*'s which soften, the transformational solution "marks" those which do not. How can we choose between these two solutions? The structural choice is a simple-minded one, relying as it does on straight economy: since fewer prepalatal *s*'s undergo softening than resist it, fewer specifications are needed in the lexicon if one marks those which soften than if one marks those which don't. Transformational grammar also relies on economy, but links it to "plausibility," defined roughly as conformity with what can be assumed to go on in the speaker's mind. The facts being what they are, any "grammatical" solution, any genuine "rule," would have to assume on the part of the speaker a highly implausible ability to make sophisticated chronological and/or etymological distinctions which require the competence of a historical linguist. Of course, the transformationalist will avail himself of such diachronic distinctions and telescope them in synchrony by postulating as many abstract entities as needed to account for synchronically unmotivated differences in behavior. Supposed to "explain" differences in phonological behavior, these entities are nothing but roundabout ways of restating the original differences. As such, they explain nothing. Thus, the transformational solution fails by its very own standard, plausibility. It is, after all, the unfashionable structural solution, which implies that speakers handle the descriptively unpredictable prepalatal *s*'s by memorization rather than generalization, that is more likely to duplicate the processes through which speakers produce correct forms.[22]

4.6 Goals

A solution which satisfies the goals of its own model should not be discredited because it does not satisfy the goals of another.

Many disputes between structuralists and transformationalists result from a failure to differentiate means from ends: a solution can be criticized because it fails to attain the ends it has set for itself or because it attains ends deemed inferior to other, more desirable, ends. One can quarrel with a solution either as an inappropriate means to its own ends or with the particular ends it seeks to achieve. Both are legitimate quarrels, but they are quarrels of a different kind: one is technical in nature, with measurable alternatives, and it questions whether the solution takes full and consistent advantage of the resources inherent in its model; the other, more abstract, is permeated by unstated value judgments about both the nature of language and human nature in general. The former are quarrels about alternative solutions, the latter about alternative models.

[22] "There are a number of examples in the literature of cases where the linguist would posit an 'elegant' solution with abstract underlying forms and ordered rules, but where the other evidence in the language shows that the native speaker's solution posits a less elegant and also a less abstract analysis." Hooper 1974, p. 160, with further references. Also to the point is Venneman's comment on difficulties encountered in generative phonology which do not arise in natural phonology: "Of course, these problems should not arise, because they are not, for all that we know, problems of language users but only of linguists committed to those models of language" (1974, p. 347).

To make a modicum of sense out of our disputes we must distinguish the two kinds of controversies and keep them apart. Ruhlen fails to do so because he can conceive of linguistic investigations only in terms of those particular goals which inform generative and transformational grammar. As a result, he is under the constant misconception that the debates he engages in are instrumental when they, in fact, presuppose hidden commitments of an axiological nature. Most of the time Ruhlen believes that he is taking issue with structural solutions as inappropriate means to mutually agreed ends, when what he is actually questioning are the goals of structuralism. More plainly, Ruhlen keeps pestering structuralists for not reaching San Francisco when, for better or for worse, they have chosen to take the way to San José. "Turn right rather than left!" may be one of two things: a technical instruction meaning "Turn right to reach San Francisco, if that's where you want to go!", or an exhortation meaning "Don't go to San José, go to San Francisco! It's so much more fun!"

These distinctions elude Ruhlen as they have eluded other transformationalists, and this is why criticism of structuralist solutions seldom contributes to the elucidation of the problems at hand. One can certainly take issue with structuralists for seeking unworthy goals, as well as for failing to reach the goals they have sought. But only confusion can come from mistaking one kind of criticism for the other, as in the abstruse pages Ruhlen devotes to "The explanatory power of phonological derivations"[23] in which he needlessly complicates the well-known developments of such forms as *creşte* "grow," from the Latin CRESCIT. Consider the following sets:

plak=i > plač=j   las=i > laš=j   kresk=i > krešt=j
plak=e > plač=e   las=e > las=e   kresk=e > krešt=e

In the first set, *k* is palatalized into *č* by both =j and =e, plač=j and plač=e, in the second *s* is palatalized into *š* by =j but not by =e, laš=j but las=e. In the third set, however, *s* seems to pattern with *k*, not with *s*, as it appears palatalized by both =j and =e, krešt=j and krešt=e. This apparent discrepancy disappears as

[23] Ruhlen 1974, pp. 180-182.

soon as the actual development is taken into account: kresk=e > kresč=e > krešč=e > krešt=e. In creṣte, s is softened not by the remote =e, but by the č which immediately follows, into which k has been softened by the following e.

These changes can be explained in terms of three rules, /ke > če/, /sč > šč/, and /šč > št/. Transformationalist injunctions notwithstanding,[24] the order of these rules need not be specified, as the third rule presupposes the second and the second the first. Stipulating the order of the rules would be redundant because the conditions of the third change are not satisfied until the second has taken place, nor those of the second before the first: /šč > št/ cannot take place because /šč/ does not exist until /sč > šč/, which in turn cannot occur because /sč/ does not exist until /ke > če/.

In *The Rumanian Verb System*, Edwards and I provided the first and third rules but skipped the second to predict the s in creṣte directly relative to the ending =e.[25] We did so in order to comply with one of the constraints imposed on us by our model: the reconstitution of all standard Rumanian forms *with a minimum of rules*. In doing so, we economized one rule at the expense of one stipulation relating to stems ending in -sk=. Now here is what Ruhlen makes of this elementary alternative:

> The generative solution I have advanced unifies the phonological process of Sibilant Palatalization. It claims that the reason s is palatalized in /krešte/ is the SAME reason it is palatalized in /lašj/ and /guštj/. Rather than constituting an anomaly in the language, /krešte/ is precisely the form we should expect once the full interaction of the phonological rules is taken into account. However, this explanation cannot be made in terms of surface structure, for it is the INTERMEDIATE segment /č/ which triggers the palatalization of /krešte/. I conclude, therefore, that investigations of Rumanian phonology which are arbitrarily limited to surface structure are bound to leave unstated important generalizations. (182)

Ruhlen seems unaware that all it takes to "unify the phonological process of Sibilant Palatalization" is to introduce the second rule and remove the restriction to stems ending in -sk=. What such high-sounding notions as "deep structure" and "surface manifestation" have to do with this simple alternative—remove a

---

[24] The programmatic statement is Chomsky and Halle 1968. Cf., for instance, King 1973. For a sounder view, cf. Koutsoudas, Sanders, and Noll 1974.
[25] Juilland and Edwards 1971, §2.335 and §4.321.

stipulation at the expense of a rule, remove a rule at the expense of a stipulation—is not easy to understand. What is readily understandable is that the structural model has the resources to account in a couple of plain paragraphs for what it took Ruhlen three abstruse pages to express in the transformational idiom.[26]

4.7 Labels

One version of the same solution should not be preferred to another because it uses different labels to refer to the same distinctions.

There are other sources of misunderstanding which suggest substantive differences when, in fact, there are none. Worth mentioning is the insidious use of different labels to refer to the same distinction, solution, or operation. This may involve referring to the same procedure as "destroying" or "capturing" depending on which model is involved; or criticizing "taxonomists" for playing sterile classification games when critics indulge in the same games under the more palatable label of "generalization";[27] or concealing exceptions, if not outright lexical treatment by ad hoc contrivances called "minor rules." Perhaps the worst kind of obfuscation is the manipulation of labels such as "deep structure" and "surface manifestation" to favor the solutions of one model to the detriment of their equivalent advanced by another.

Ruhlen takes us to task for having contended that a good structural morphology ought to be largely convertible into a transformational morphology, and vice versa. He especially objects to our use of the verb "generate" when we argue that "by combining 'our' entities in accordance with 'our' rules, any and all standard Rumanian verb forms can be generated more economically than by resorting to entities and rules presupposed by other analyses."[28]

---

[26] On the same point, cf. Rosetti 1974.
[27] "There may be those who honestly don't want to explain things—they just want to classify sound patterns and engage in pure taxonomy. I can't say I know any card-carrying taxonomist, but if I were to meet one I would respect him and his philosophy though I disagreed with it. But it is difficult to have respect for certain others who profess to be interested in explaining sound patterns but in fact are secret taxonomists." Ohala 1974, p. 251.
[28] Juilland and Edwards 1971, p. 42.

However, the meaning which J & E assign to the word 'generate' and the sense in which the term is used in transformational studies are fundamentally different, and this discrepancy serves more to obscure the basic difference between the two models than point out true similarities. In short, J & E proceed as follows: The surface representations of the verbal forms are first chopped up via the familiar procedures of segmentation, identification, and classification. Once this is done, rules are supplied which, in effect, put the pieces back together, or, in J & E words, generate "all standard Rumanian verb forms." "Generate" thus signifies for J & E a relationship between SURFACE morphemes and surface verb forms. In transformational grammar, however, "generate" is used quite differently, specifying a relationship between an ABSTRACT UNDERLYING FORM and its various SURFACE MANIFESTATIONS. This then is the basic difference between J & E's structuralist model and the generative approach. The former is primarily concerned with relationships holding on the surface, while the latter concentrates on the relationship between two DIFFERENT levels, one abstract, the other concrete. (179-180)

To understand what Ruhlen means in concrete terms, consider any morpheme which occurs in more than one shape, e.g., the inflection of the Present Indicative 3 of the 1st conjugation which exhibits one of two endings, =ă or =e, *cîntă* /kɨnt=ə/ but *taie* /taj=e/. As =e occurs in postpalatal positions and =ă in all other positions, the two can be interpreted as allomorphs of the same inflectional morphemes symbolized by = {æ}.[29] In a static formulation, the allomorph =e occurs, or is selected by, stems ending in a palatal, the allomorph =ă by all other stems; a dynamic formulation would state that the ending =ă is converted or transformed into =e by stems ending in a palatal.

Contrary to what Ruhlen believes, "generate" in *The Rumanian Verb System* does not mean merely "a relationship between surface morphemes," for it also signifies the relationship between the underlying morpheme = {æ} and its allomorphic manifestations =ă and =e. Nor is it true that the structural model is "primarily concerned with relationships holding on the surface, while the [generative model] concentrates on the relationship between two DIFFERENT levels, one abstract, the other concrete,"

---

[29] The same applies to other inflectional morphemes which occur in more than one shape, e.g., the Imperfect ={Em etc.}, post-palatal =am etc., other positions =eam etc; or the Gerund ={Ind}, post-palatal =ind, other positions =înd. It also applies to suffixes such as -{ez}=, post-palatal -az=, other positions -eaz=; or -{ESK}=, post-palatal -asĸ=, other positions -easĸ=; etc. For an exhaustive inventory of such variants, cf. Juilland and Edwards 1971, §2.33

for there are also two different levels in the structural approach, one abstract, the level of morphemes, the other concrete, the level of morphs. At least in this context, the distinction between "abstract underlying forms" and their "surface manifestations" looks suspiciously like the old structural distinction between "emes" which, as abstractions, never occur, and their "allos," which do. This fundamental equivalence is disguised by the re-labelling of morphs as "surface morphemes," which converts old-fashioned morphemes into "deep structure morphemes."

It is also difficult to understand Ruhlen's claim that the structural model does not recognize abstract underlying forms, when its main objective is to provide morpholexical transcripts such as {kɨnT=a}. These morpholexical transcripts are the counterparts of lexical representations and are to be verified in the same way, i.e., by combining stems symbolized as {kɨnT}= with endings symbolized as ={a} in accordance with the rules formulated in the grammar. As betrayed by his description of our procedure, Ruhlen has been led astray by the preliminary section called "Analysis," which provides a step-by-step justification of the procedures which abstract from surface manifestations the symbols used in the morpholexical transcriptions. He describes our procedure as one in which "the surface representations of verbal forms are first chopped up via the familiar procedures of segmentation, identification, and classification," when the last two operations have nothing to do with dividing, as only segmentation divides. Identification reduces variants to invariants, i.e., the "chopped up" surface manifestations or "allos" to entities of a first degree of abstraction called "emes," while classification groups invariants into larger entities of a second degree of abstraction called "classes." Far from "putting the pieces back together," our rules derive concrete forms from the abstract symbols which constitute morpholexical transcripts.

In conclusion, whatever the specific sources of these conflicting solutions, it is important to distinguish between extraneous factors and intrinsic differences rooted in the resources and constraints of the models themselves. On closer inspection, many disputes between structuralists and transformationalists turn out to be quarrels which, because they focus on alternatives conditioned by incidental factors and circumstances, have little to do with the descriptive and explanatory powers of the rival models. At least on morphological grounds, the differences between structural and transformational grammar have been greatly exaggerated.

5

CONCLUSIONS

This essay was prompted by two different but related claims: a specific claim, that Rumanian =ea and =e verbs are better grouped as marked and unmarked subsets of the same conjugation rather than assigned, as in *The Rumanian Verb System*, to different conjugations; and a more general claim, that Edwards and I ended up with the wrong solution because we followed an outdated structural approach, while Ruhlen proposed the right solution because he had the benefit of a superior transformational model.

In rebuttal, we tried to show why =ea verbs and =e verbs are better assigned to different conjugations; and we argued that the choice between the two solutions has nothing to do with the "rival" structural and transformational approaches to grammar. Let us enumerate some of the *real* issues upon which the choice hinges:

1. Are superclasses a "special apparatus" improvised to rescue relationships destroyed at an earlier stage of the analysis? Or are they an indispensable component of every system of classification, on a par with classes and subclasses by which they are presupposed? (§2.1)

2. Should similarities between members of different classes be ignored in a description which takes into account dissimilarities between members of the same class? (§2.2)

3. Can the solution which accounts for similarities between =ea and =e verbs by assigning them to the same conjugation be generalized to account for similarities between verbs assigned to different classes? (§2.3)

4. Can a classificatory model which excludes superclasses do justice to the relationships between members of different classes? (§2.3)

5. How many forms, three or six, differ accentually between =ea verbs and =e verbs? (§3.21)

6. Are =ea verbs a marked subset of =e verbs? (§3.22)

7. Are =e verbs statistically stronger than =e verbs, or is it the other way around? In answering such questions, should one rely on dictionary frequency or on textual frequency? (§3.221)

8. Do =ea verbs tend to be assimilated by =e verbs? (§3.222)

9. Is there a trend from the =ea set to the =e set or from =e to =ea? Are there shifts in both directions? (§3.2221)

10. Do statistical considerations have any bearing on the answer to the preceding questions? Should one rely on written or spoken evidence for answering such questions? (§3.2221)

11. Are *rămîne* and *place* analogical reshapings of *rămînea* and *plăcea*? Are they hypercorrections? Are they descendants of the Vulgar Latin REMÁNERE and PLÁCERE? (§3.2222)

12. Is the difference between coexistent forms like *rămînea* and *rămîne* or *plăcea* and *place* chronological or sociocultural? Can we infer from their coexistence anything about the evolution of the two sets in the future? (§3.2222)

13. Are there genuine transitions from one conjugation to the other or only shifts in accentual patterns? (§3.2222)

14. Of the two changes, =ea > =e and =e > =ea, which is analogical and which hypercorrective? (§3.2223)

15. Are accentual differences between verbs like *aluneca* and *alerga* on a par with accentual differences between verbs like *vedea* and *face*? Should these differences play identical roles in the classification? (§3.23)

16. Are properties symbolized in the morpholexical representations morphological or lexical? Can these properties provide a basis for morphological classification? (§3.31)

17. Can sigmatism be predicted relative to the last two phonemes of the stem? Is Agard's rule a genuine rule or is it a covert form of listing? (§3.32)

Ruhlen gives the wrong answers to most of these questions, which explains why his solution is wrong. Or vice versa: he begins by committing himself to the wrong solution and, consequently, asks the wrong questions. In any case, "right" or "wrong" answers have little to do with the model used: if the linguist has all the facts and interprets them correctly, the right solution is likely to emerge regardless of "approach." Whether solutions are expressed in structural or transformational idiom is largely a question of style, not of substance.

In the subtle interplay between theory and practice, a tendency to overestimate good models to the detriment of good solutions is responsible for many of the misunderstandings which have been plaguing us. In other words, there is a tendency to assume that good solutions are derived from good models rather than to view good models as extrapolations from good solutions. Combined with a Manichaean outlook which takes it for granted that structuralism is bad and transformationalism good, this misconception leads to a belief that for every (implicitly bad) structural solution there must be an (implicitly good) alternative which transformational maieutic will bring to the fore. Ruhlen's trouble is that, blinded by this Manichaean vision, he cannot recognize a good solution when he sees one especially when it bears the trappings of structuralism. And because in most instances traditionalists and structuralists had the first crack at discovering the right solutions, Ruhlen has only leftovers to work with to prove the superiority of his approach. No wonder, given such unfortunate circumstances, that he has so much difficulty making the transformational case.

I do not mean to suggest that there are no significant differences between the two approaches, nor do I mean that transformational grammar may not be superior in certain areas (especially syntax). I am suggesting, however, that the evidence will have to be sought elsewhere, outside of Rumanian morphology, if not outside of morphology in general. In our view, structural morphology is equal to transformational morphology provided that one understands by structuralism a doctrine which grew out of Saussure's *Cours*,[1] Sapir's *Language*,[2] Jakobson's *Prinzipien*,[3] Trubetskoj's *Grundzüge*,[4] Hjelmslev's *Omkring*,[5] or Martinet's

---

[1] de Saussure 1916.
[2] Sapir 1921.
[3] Jakobson 1928.
[4] Trubetskoy 1939.
[5] Hjelmslev 1943.

Économie,[6] and not the desiccated post-Bloomfieldian descriptivism, an easy strawman for transformationalists.

By now I do feel emboldened enough to hazard the proposition that certain basic postulates of transformational grammar are unrealistic and unworkable, while their structural counterparts are sounder. We have seen that certain forms are subject to palatalization while others are not, that certain prepalatal consonants soften while others resist the assimilatory influence of the following sound. Confronted with this situation, transformationalists assume that because native speakers without etymological knowledge manage to keep the two kinds of forms apart, and that because children without historical insight easily learn which prepalatal consonants soften and which do not, there must be a synchronic connection, a generalization, a rule, which facilitates the distinction and helps produce correct forms. Structuralists, on the other hand, assume that in many instances there are no such rules, that native speakers learn the distinction by trial and error, i.e., by lexical rather than grammatical means: children, by making mistakes and by being corrected, learn which forms are which. Transformational rules notwithstanding, natives solve many such problems by memorization, not by generalization.[7]

Furthermore, linguists of a more traditional bent contend that even when certain synchronic rules happen to work, they are the result of accidental conjunctions which fail to reveal the true mechanisms they are meant to explain. The main distinction which governs Rumanian palatalizations is between inherited stock and neologisms or loan words, between forms present in the language when palatalization occurred and forms created or adopted after the phenomenon ceased being active. Nothing prevents us from assuming that because of early phonological erosion—loss of unstressed vowels or intervocalic consonants, simplification of clusters, reduction of hiatus, etc.—inherited

---

[6] Martinet 1955.
[7] "The first principle of morphology is Saussure's principle of *arbitrariness*. The psychological relationship between phonetic and semantic representations in language is arbitrary. In language acquisition, these relationships—because they are arbitrary—are all initially memorized. Later in acquisition, rules are learned which account for certain regularities in these arbitrary relationships. Rules may reduce the degree of memorization, but do not eliminate it entirely." Skousen 1974, p. 319.

forms shrank to a maximum of two syllables, whereas loan words have at least three; or that inherited stock words, through the loss of posttonic vowels, came to bear the stress on the last syllable, as opposed to neologisms which are accented on a syllable other than the last; etc. In such circumstances, it would be tempting to link resistance to palatalization (or to any change which preceded the creation or adoption of neologisms) to one of the features which characterize borrowings or derivations, e.g., prepalatal consonants of monosyllabic words undergo softening, those of polysyllabic words resist it; prepalatal consonants of oxytones soften, those of paroxytones or proparoxytones do not. Not only would such synchronic rules be descriptively valid, speakers could actually rely on them to determine which consonants to soften and which not. Still the implication of such rules—that monosyllabism or oxytony inhibits palatalization—would be misleading insofar as there is no real connection between these phenomena.

Since there is no necessary reason why loan words should be consistently marked relative to inherited forms—languages abound in which they are not—there could well be a situation in which regular and irregular forms would be descriptively indistinguishable. The tendency to assume that there *must* be a synchronic connection which facilitates such distinctions only exacerbates the situation: rules are contrived to "grammaticalize" lexical distinctions through a plethora of "minor," "crazy," or "pseudo" rules which assume that speakers proceed by generalization when they, in fact, handle such distinctions by inventorization.

This brings into focus another assumption about the relationships which obtain between rules, intuitions, and explanations. Transformationalists generally take it for granted that good rules explain native intuitions rooted in the deeper mechanisms of the language. This fruitful assumption has allowed for a more satisfying linguistics which aspires to explain, a refreshing change from the pasteurized structuralism which considered explanations nothing but "loose talk."[8] But however sound, this assumption must be viewed with caution inasmuch as intuitions can be at the same time true and false, that is, synchronically

---

[8] Joos 1950, p. 280. On this point, cf. Juilland 1967, pp. 357-358.

valid but diachronically unfounded. The example mentioned above offers a good illustration of the dangers involved: native speakers may feel it "in their bones" that there is a connection between resistance to palatalization and polysyllabism or oxytony, a "true" intuition insofar as it may produce correct forms. But such a descriptively accurate and generatively effective intuition suggests a causal nexus between palatalization and number of syllables or position of stress when the real explanation lies deep below the synchronic "surface" and way beyond the scope of achronic probing, structural *or* transformational. We are confronted with different conceptions of what constitutes an explanation: transformationalists strive to explain how correct forms are produced by the speaker, how they are actualized in speech, how they come into being. European structuralists, on the other hand, have tried to understand how forms came to be as they are. Rather than explain how speakers produce forms, linguists who try to bridge the gap between structure and evolution see it as their task to understand how it came about that the speakers produce what they are producing.[9]

Both structuralists and transformationalists ought to face the fact that certain descriptively motivated features are historically arbitrary and that certain diachronic developments are no longer traceable in synchrony. It is especially important to realize that what is true is not necessarily real. When modern linguists banned historical insights from descriptive investigations, they cut themselves off from the diachronic sources which condition synchronic states. The structuralist breakthrough was achieved at the price of severing all connections with the evolutionary realities which underlie synchronic configurations. Because of their anti-explanatory bias, American structuralists have been willing to accept the severe methodological limitation originally imposed by Saussure's synchronic/diachronic antinomy, a limitation partly inherited by generative phonology and only recently challenged by advocates of natural phonology.[10]

The challenge issued by the proponents of this new school suggests that, after years of success, the time has come for orthodox transformationalists to reexamine some of their axioms,

[9] Kiparski 1968.
[10] Hooper 1973.

e.g., those rooted in the syntactic beginnings of transformational phonology and morphology. Just as the structural approach to grammar, which bore the marks of its phonological origins, was distorted by efforts to squeeze morphological and syntactic data into Procrustrean categories first established on phonological grounds,[11] so the transformational approach to morphology and phonology may have been unduly influenced by the overextension of hypotheses which had proven useful in the analysis and interpretation of syntactic data. By reconsidering some of the basic assumptions of Chomskyan linguistics, transformationalists may relinquish some of their more extravagant claims; they may also arrive at a more concrete and realistic view of phonology and morphology, thus bringing them closer to the practices of their traditionalist and structuralist forerunners. As a matter of fact, such a reconciliation seems well underway, as evidenced by the cogent, persuasive and, in my opinion, long overdue arguments of the advocates of natural phonology.[12] But as one who has witnessed some of the questionable developments hailed until recently as auguries of a new linguisitc era, I am disappointed to see so much talent expended on undoing the harm perpetrated in the name of a more progressive linguistics. That the scholarship deployed "to correct faults in the theory of generative phonology epitomized by Chomsky and Halle's *Sound Pattern of English* must be defined in this negative way"[13] is understandable. Schane's complaint that "some of the 'natural phonology' proposals . . . actually constitute a return to pre-generative times"[14] goes straight to the heart of the matter.

Now I've been proven wrong in the past and I expect to be proven wrong in the future, which is to say that although past the age of conversions, I wouldn't mind trying. But if I am to go through the labors of a late conversion, I'd like to make sure that I am converting to a better religion, and brackets and branches alone won't do it, though the promise of fresh insights and genuine discoveries may. What I expect from a new morphological model is that it teach me something new about the language

---

[11] Juilland and Roceric 1975, pp. 26-31.
[12] Bruck, Fox, and Lagaly 1974.
[13] Schane 1974, p. 299.
[14] Darden 1974, p. 1.

I'm studying rather than a new way of saying what I already know. To put it more defensively, I hope that the case against structural morphology can be built on arguments more solid and more persuasive than those advanced in the study I have challenged. The only real differences I could find between the "rival approaches" are stylistic rather than substantive. And though style *is* important, it is crucial to know when we quarrel about style and when we argue about grammar.

BIBLIOGRAPHY

Bach, Emmon and Robert T. Harms. 1972. "How Do Languages Get Crazy Rules?" *Linguistic Change and Generative Theory*. Bloomington.
Bloomfield, Leonard. 1933. *Language*. New York.
Bruck, Anthony, Robert A. Fox, and Michael W. Lagaly, eds. 1974. *Papers from the Parasession on Natural Phonology*. Chicago.
Chomsky, Noam, and Morris T. Halle. 1963. *Sound Pattern of English*. New York.
Darden, Bill. 1974. Introduction. *Papers from the Parasession on Natural Phonology*. Pp. 1-7.
Felix, Jiří. 1964. "Classification des verbes roumains." *Filologica Pragensia* 7:291-299.
Grandgent, Charles. 1934. *An Introduction to Vulgar Latin*. New York.
Guţu Romalo, Valeria. 1968. *Morfologie Structurală a Limbii Române*. Bucureşti.
———. 1972. *Corectitudine şi Greşeală*. Bucureşti.
Hjelmslev, Louis. 1943. *Omkring Sprogteoriens Grundloeggelse*. København.
Hooper, Joan. 1973. "Aspects of Natural Phonology." University of California, Los Angeles (dissertation).
———. 1974. "Rule Morphologization in Natural Generative Phonology." *Papers from the Parasession on Natural Phonology*. Pp. 160-170.
Hyman, Larry. 1975. *Introduction to Phonology*. New York.
Iordan, Iorgu. 1947. *Limba Română Actuală: O Gramatică a "Greşelilor."* Bucureşti.
Izzo, Herbert. 1976. "Pre-Latin Change and Sound Changes in Romance: The Case of Old Spanish /h/." Ann Arbor (unpublished paper).

Jakobson, Roman. 1928. "Prinzipien der historischen Phonologie." *Travaux du Cercle Linguistique de Prague* 4:1.
Joos, Martin. 1950. "Description of Language Design." *Journal of the Acoustic Society of America* 22:701-708.
Juilland, Alphonse. 1953. "A Bibliography of Diachronic Phonemics." *Word* 9:198-208.
―――――. 1969. "Perspectives du Structuralisme évolutif." *Linguistic Studies Presented to André Martinet*. Pp. 350-361.
―――――. 1972. "Entry Words: Grammars and Dictionaries." *Papers in Linguistics and Phonetics to the Memory of Pierre Delattre*. The Hague-Paris. Pp. 253-271.
Juilland, Alphonse, and Eugene Elliott. 1957. "Perspectives of Linguistic Science." *Monograph Series on Languages and Linguistics*. No. 9, pp. 170-200.
Juilland, Alphonse, and Paul M. Edwards. 1965. *Frequency Dictionary of Rumanian Words*. The Hague.
―――――. 1971. *The Rumanian Verb System*. The Hague.
Juilland, Alphonse, and Hans-Heinrich Lieb. 1968. *Klasse und Klassifikation in der Sprachwissenschaft*. The Hague.
Juilland, Alphonse, and Alexandra Roceric. 1975. *The Decline of the Word*. Saratoga.
King, Robert T. 1973. "In Defense of Extrinsic Ordering." *Indiana Conference on Extrinsic Ordering*. Bloomington.
Kiparsky, Paul. 1968. "Linguistic Universals and Linguistic Change." *Universals in Linguistic Theory*. New York. Pp. 346-374.
Koutsoudas, A., G. Sanders, and C. Noll. 1974. "On the Application of Phonological Rules." *Language* 50:1-28.
Martinet, André. 1955. *Économie des Changements Phonétiques*. Berne.
Ohala, John J. 1974. "Phonetic Explanation in Phonology." *Papers from the Parasession on Natural Phonology*. Pp. 346-374.
Pop, Ghiţă. 1911. *Taschewörterbuch der Rumänischen und Deutschen Sprachen*. Berlin.
Puşcariu, Sextil. 1940. *Limba Română*. Vol. I: *Privire Generală*. Bucureşti.
Rosetti, Alexandru. 1974. "Sur la 'Phonologie Générative'." *Revue Romaine de Linguistique* 19:579.
Ruhlen, Merritt. 1973. "Rumanian Phonology." Stanford University (dissertation).
―――――. 1973b. "Despre nivelul fonematic în limba românä." *Studii şi Cercetări Lingvistice* 24:170-186.
―――――. 1973-74. "On the Importance of Minor Rules in the Description of Rumanian Verbs." *Romance Philology* 26:36-45.
―――――. 1974. "Two Rival Approaches to Rumanian Grammar: Classical Structuralism vs. Transformational Analysis." *Romance Philology* 28:178-190.

Sapir, Edward. 1921. *Language*. New York.
Saussure, Ferdinand de. 1916. *Cours de Linguistique Générale*. Paris.
Schane, Sanford A. 1974. "How Abstract Is Abstract?" *Papers from the Parasession on Natural Phonology*. Pp. 297-317.
Skousen, Royal. 1974. "An Explanatory Theory of Morphology." *Papers from the Parasession on Natural Phonology*. Pp. 318-327.
Stockwell, Robert P., and Ronald S. Macaulay, eds. 1971. *Linguistic Change and Generative Theory*. Bloomington and London.
Trubetskoj, Nikolaj S. 1939. *Grundzüge der Phonologie*. Praag.
Väänänen, Veikko. 1963. *Introduction au Latin Vulgaire*. Paris.
Vennemann, Theo. 1974. "Words and Syllables in Natural Generative Grammar." *Papers from the Parasession on Natural Phonology*. Pp. 346-347.
———, and Terence H. Wilbur. 1972. *Schuchardt, the Neogrammarians, and the Transformational Theory of Phonological Change: Four Essays*. Frankfurt am Main.

BOOKS AND MONOGRAPHS
BY ALPHONSE JUILLAND

Structural Relations: Outline of a General Theory. 1961. 62 pp.

The English Verb System. With James Macris. 1962. 81 pp.

Louisiana French Grammar: Phonology, Morphology, and Syntax. With Marylin Conwell. 1964. 207 pp.

Frequency Dictionary of Spanish Words. With Eugenio Chang-Rodriguez. 1964. lxxvii + 500 pp.

Dictionnaire inverse de la langue française. 1965. lx + 503 pp.

Frequency Dictionary of Rumanian Words. With P.M.H. Edwards. 1966. lxxiv + 513 pp.

Linguistic Studies Presented to André Martinet on the Occasion of His Sixtieth Birthday. Editor. 3 vols. 1967-70. 1,465 pp.

Klasse und Klassifikation in der Sprachwissenschaft. With Hans-Heinrich Lieb. 1968. 75 pp.

Frequency Dictionary of French Words. With Dorothy Brodin and Catherine Davidovitch. 1970. lxxv + 503 pp.

The Rumanian Verb System. With P.M.H. Edwards. 1971. 220 pp.

The Linguistic Concept of Word: Analytic Bibliography. With Alexandra Roceric. 1972. 118 pp.

Frequency Dictionary of Italian Words. With Vincenzo Traversa. 1973. lxxii + 519 pp.

Essai pour une histoire structurale du phonétisme français. With André Haudricourt. 2nd ed. 1974. 135 pp.

The Decline of the Word. With Alexandra Roceric. 1975. 62 pp.

Linguistic Studies Presented to Joseph Greenberg on the Occasion of His Sixtieth Birthday. Editor. 3 vols. 1977. 636 pp.

Transformational and Structural Morphology. 1977. 78 pp.

LIBRARY OF DAVIDSON COLLEGE

Books on regular loan may be checked out for **two weeks**. Books must be presented at the Circulation Desk in order to be renewed.

A fine is charged after date due.

Special books are subject to special regulations at the discretion of the library staff.